by the same author

He Died Old

HE DIED OLD
Mithradates Eupator, King of Pontus

by

ALFRED DUGGAN

'Mithridates, he died old'
—A. E. HOUSMAN, *A Shropshire lad*

FABER AND FABER

24 Russell Square

London

First published in mcmlviii
by Faber and Faber Limited
24 Russell Square London W.C.1
Printed in Great Britain by
Latimer Trend & Co Ltd Plymouth
All rights reserved

© *Alfred Duggan*
1958

Prologue

We of the west remember the Romans as bringers of civilization. Gaul, Britain and Spain were made by Rome. Rome taught us to live by law, to obey our rulers, to dwell together in the crowded confines of the city. Without Rome we might be coolies ruled by brigands; as some industrious and productive nations, who never endured the Roman discipline, have remained throughout history nothing more than coolies, looking for brigands to rule them.

But that is not the whole story of Rome. In the course of their amazing expansion the Romans collided with peoples of an older culture, peoples who had already learned the good life and could live it; in everything but military skill superior to the blunt, uncouth farmers of central Italy. To the Hellenized east Rome could offer nothing, nothing but the grasping hand of the tax-farmer and the blood-drinking sword of the legionary. Especially in Asia Minor the Romans were resisted, by civilized men who regarded them as savages. This is a study of the greatest hero of that resistance.

Asia Minor appears on the map as a solid undivided peninsula, and for many centuries it has formed part of a single state. We cannot but think of it as a unit. In fact it is three very different lands. The interior is a plateau, rolling grassland cut by rare streams, or dotted with stagnant lakes of brackish water; in appearance and in truth an extension of the steppe of central Asia. This plateau is bounded on every side by mountains, thickly wooded and seamed with steep ravines; to north, west and south the mountains descend to a coastal plain of varying extent. The plateau is scourged by the summer heat and winter cold of inner Asia; in the forested mountains, which

9

nowhere attain the altitude of perpetual snow, the seasons are much as in the Pyrenees; the coastal plains, where vines and olives ripen, blaze in Mediterranean sunshine. The plateau runs continuously from Armenia to the Hellespont, and the mountains form a girdle interrupted only by rare passes; in many places these mountains come right down to the sea, so that the coastal districts are cut off into compartments. It has always been very difficult to travel along the southern shore, from the Troad to Cilicia, as the armies of our crusading ancestors discovered to their cost.

Because of these geographical factors the neolithic farmers who settled on the central plateau, about seven thousand years ago, quickly formed themselves into states of considerable area; the mountaineers, living scattered in deep valleys, grew accustomed to paying reluctant and nominal allegiance to a distant tyrant; but each segment of the coastal plain went its separate way. The geographical unit of Asia Minor was in the main a single political unit; but with a fringe of independent cantons by the shore.

Civilization came early to this land, separated only by the range of Taurus from Syria, one of the cradles of civilization. Long before Achilles sailed to Troy, heroes who wielded bronze swords and drove two-horsed chariots ruled an industrious corn-growing peasantry on the plateau. But it seems that these heroes were always a conquering aristocracy. They built palaces, temples, fortresses, and mighty tombs which were the seed of the most surprising legends; but they did not build cities, for they were too few. A single noble family ruled each farming village from its hilltop castle. The peasants, of inferior race, were not worthy to live with their masters behind a common wall.

The belief was universal in antiquity that iron was first smelted in Asia Minor. There was gold in the streams and silver in the mountainsides. Three thousand years ago the mailed chieftains of the plateau, now armed with iron swords and iron spearheads, drank wine from golden cups in splendid stone palaces. About this time the first Greek colonists, founders of the culture which we inherit, were creeping eastward from headland to headland in their frail crowded ships.

Greeks occupied the coastal plains to the south, founding a

Prologue

separate city on each patch of level cornland. Each city was a completely sovereign independent state; but the Greeks felt themselves bound by ties of common blood and common language, and often they formed leagues of allied cities against the foreigners who ruled the inland. The foreigners were of course known as 'barbarians'; not because they were savages (on the material plane their culture was richer than that of the Greek cities), but because they did not speak Greek. A barbarian is any man who makes a noise like bar-bar instead of answering in the tongue all proper men can understand.

This wealthy and prosperous land attracted the regard of the even wealthier and more powerful tyrants who reigned to the eastward of Taurus. The Persians were warriors and nothing but warriors; they lived by conquering men of a higher civilization and making them pay taxes. The Great King of Persia swept westward to the Hellespont, until by the fifth century B.C. he ruled the whole inland country of Asia Minor, and the self-governing Greek cities of the coast thought it prudent to pay him tribute. For more than a century the peninsula was united under a single ruler. Trade flourished; the cities pushed out colonies northward to the shores of the Euxine; mighty temples, served by thousands of bondsmen, made famous the remote inland valleys. Political exiles from European Greece, riding along the Royal Road to seek help from the King of Kings in far-off Persepolis, were astonished at the wealth and fruitfulness they saw.

In the fourth century there came from the west the Macedonians, Greek warriors using Greek arms and Greek tactics; but their spearmen were peasants, more formidable than Greek city-dwellers, and they were led by a general of genius. When Alexander the Great died in 322 B.C. (and that is the first date we need note in this essay) Asia Minor formed part of his great empire, which stretched from the Adriatic to the Oxus.

At once every Asiatic whose trade was war, that is to say every Asiatic above the social level of the poorest villager, saw that Greek ways must be best. To be prosperous and successful you must live like a Greek. Alexander and his generals founded Greek cities all over the Empire. Their example was copied by local chieftains, until every patch of level cornland west of the Euphrates supported a walled town, complete with market-place for political discussion, columned temples dedicated to the Homeric gods, a gymnasium for athletes and a theatre for variety shows, if not for truly classical stage plays. The citizens of these towns were known by Greek names, and most of them were descended in the male line from some Greek soldier of Alexander's army; though their female ancestors may have been barbarian. The townsmen went busily through the motions of being Greek citizens: voting after hearing political speeches, taking exercise naked, drilling with the Greek spear and shield. But often the only outcome of their voting was another statue of the local barbarian ruler, and if they were menaced by war they hired mercenaries from the mountains and themselves stayed in their shops. This imported Greek culture was a pale imitation of the real thing, and it was spread very thin.

As soon as Alexander was dead his generals fought among themselves for his crown. These generals fought bitterly enough, since the stake was the greatest prize in the world. But their soldiers were not deeply engaged, for neither patriotism nor political principle divided them. The wars brought sudden changes of fortune for the leaders, but they were waged under humane rules and did little damage to the countryside. It was taken for granted that no city would resist an invader, unless it was garrisoned by the troops of a rival general; therefore cities were never sacked. It was taken for granted that mercenary soldiers would surrender, and probably join the other army, if caught at a disadvantage; therefore quarter was always granted to armies defeated in the field. Rulers who fought for power, soldiers who fought for pay, did not kill the goose which laid the golden eggs.

These meaningless and half-hearted wars continued for a generation; about 280 B.C. they were complicated by the arrival of a horde of savage Gauls, who had wandered from the upper Danube in search of plunder. Presently these Gauls, worn out by costly victories, were induced to settle in the poorest land in the peninsula, the desolate plains bordering the central lakes. Nobody else wanted these plains earnestly enough to fight for them against warlike savages. In future the central basin was known as Galatia.

By 200 B.C. Asia Minor, now much divided, had achieved a measure of political stability. It had crystallized into the following independent states:

Prologue

The south-west formed the Kingdom of Pergamum, a well-governed and prosperous realm, deeply penetrated by Greek culture. The city of Pergamum, the capital, was famous for the strength of its fortifications and the splendour of its palaces. There a new writing material was manufactured, called 'parchment' after the scene of its invention; the smooth enduring sheets, made from the interior membrane of the sheep, were the best writing surface known to antiquity. Parchment did not tear so easily as the fragile paper of the Nile, and it was much cheaper than the leather on which formal documents had earlier been inscribed. Pergamum, a centre of the book trade, became also a seat of learning. The ruling dynasty was composed of cultivated and humane Greeks. They drew taxes from their peasants, and gave them nothing in return, after the immemorial pattern of oriental kingship; but they were enlightened patrons of art and letters, generous benefactors to stray literary men from Greece proper. If there had to be Hellenistic Kings at all, though there is not very much to be said for them, the rulers of Pergamum were the best specimens of their type.

The ancient Greek cities on the shores of the Propontis and the Aegean, Cyzicus, Lampsacus, Ephesus, remained in name free and independent republics; but their ruling corporations always prudently fell in with the wishes of the King of Pergamum.

Eastward from Ephesus, the southern shore of Asia Minor is cut up into pockets of plain divided from one another by mountain ranges reaching to the sea. Some of these formed the colonial empire of Rhodes, a naval power which was at that time the only ancient Greek city-state still enjoying a true independence; some owed a doubtful allegiance to the far-off Kings of Egypt or Cyprus; some, particularly in Cilicia, had relapsed into anarchy as shore bases for pirates.

Beyond the dangerous Cilician coast lay Syria, where law and order prevailed; for Syria was the land of the Great King, the King of Kings. There had always been a Great King somewhere to the east of Asia Minor, ever since the Assyrian came down like a wolf on the fold. The Seleucids who now reigned in Antioch were not so powerful as their predecessors; they had already lost Persia to the Parthians who now menaced Mesopotamia. But it was part of the natural order that there should

13

Prologue

be a Great King, and the Seleucids were the only claimants to the title. It was accorded to them by long custom.

Due east from Pergamum dwelt the Gauls, on stony plains beside desolate salt lakes. These Gauls, so far from home, still kept their native tongue and some fragments of their tribal organization. But they had marched under war-chiefs, not under hereditary Kings, and they lacked an undisputed royal house. They were ruled by magnates called Tetrarchs, though often there were more than four of them. As a community they had accepted defeat; Gallic soldiers enlisted as mercenaries in every Hellenistic army, but Gallic war-bands no longer went out to plunder at large.

To the north-east of Pergamum, inland from the Propontis and the western shores of the Euxine, was the prosperous and civilized Greek Kingdom of Bithynia, with Nicomedia as its capital. In power and culture this was the only rival to Pergamum, and, like Pergamum, it was fringed by nominally independent Greek city-states. In all the land west of Galatia the townsmen and the land-owning nobles spoke Greek, lived after the Greek manner, and thought of themselves as Hellenes; though they had inherited much barbarian blood.

Eastward of Bithynia, beyond the river Halys, lay the twin realms of northern and southern Cappadocia. They differed from the other Kingdoms in that they were not of Greek origin. Their royal houses, who may have been related, claimed descent from Persian satraps who had been ruling in those parts when Alexander invaded Asia; it was said that their ancestors had gone over to the invader, and as a reward had been confirmed in their governments. They made an even prouder claim; they said that these perfidious satraps had been cadets of the royal house of Persia, and that in consequence the blood of the great Darius flowed in their veins. Proud of this ancestry, they used Persian names instead of Greek, and in religion kept up the ancient rituals of Persia.

There is nothing impossible in this pedigree, though it cannot be verified. Some Persian nobles did in fact serve Alexander, and some of them were rewarded with provinces; the Persian King of Kings kept numerous concubines, and it is likely that his less-important sons would be made satraps of outlying districts.

14

Prologue

Southern Cappadocia, between the upper Halys and the Cilician mountains, was a poor and unimportant land of wooded hills and scattered pastures. It was the most purely Asiatic part of the peninsula, a realm without cities, inhabited by barbarous herdsmen. Northern Cappadocia had been in origin a realm of the same kind; until it expanded northward to control the wealthy and cultured Greek cities which lined the south-eastern shore of the Euxine. These cities lay in fertile plains; on the hills which rose southward to the central plateau valuable timber grew above mines of rich ore. Northern Cappadocia, once it had taken in the adjoining seaboard, became rich and important. In fact this northern seaboard was so much the most valuable part of the land that presently it gave its name to the whole. Henceforth northern Cappadocia was known as the Kingdom of Pontus, for Pontus was another Greek name for the Euxine.

The annals of Pontus were computed from an era beginning in 302 B.C., which was believed to be the year of the Kingdom's foundation. This date cannot be verified, but it seems plausible; Alexander died in 322, and after that twenty years of anarchy was the fate of nearly every province in his dominions. Between 302 and 132 seven Kings ruled, of whom five bore the name Mithradates. Other Hellenistic Kings chose Greek names and did their best to behave like Greeks, even when in fact they possessed very little tincture of Greek blood; the Kings of Pontus emphasized that they were different from their neighbours. They were not Greek newcomers, but a dynasty of ancient Persian royal stock; and they proved it by using noble, outlandish Persian names.

Their manner of life was partly Greek and partly Persian, as is shown more especially in their domestic arrangements. Each King collected a large seraglio according to the Persian custom, to ensure a plentiful supply of royal children. But each King also married one special Queen, usually the daughter of another monarch; and her sons, if she bore any, would come first in the line of succession. Great ladies were prominent in Hellenistic public life. It was not unusual for a King to reign jointly with his Queen, issuing decrees which bore her name as well as his; and though in general a daughter could not hold the crown in her own right, a Queen-mother by custom acted as regent for

an infant King. Every royal marriage was an important diplomatic event, and the Queen-consort, even while she shared her
husband with a troop of concubines, was one of the most
influential figures at any Hellenistic court.

The royal Persians who ruled in Pontus were socially the
equals of any Greek ruling house. The first four Kings of the
dynasty married Seleucid princesses, daughters of the Great
King who was also the standard-bearer of Greek culture. Greek
was of course the household language of these sons of Greek
mothers, and as private individuals they ate and drank and
bathed like any other prosperous Greek. But a King of Pontus
seated on his throne, the tiara round his brow, was seen by his
subjects as the legitimate heir of Xerxes and Darius; while the
Great King of Antioch was only the successor of a lucky
Macedonian general.

The land of Pontus thus contained two separate cultures. On
the central plateau, between the Halys and the Lycus, a con-
servative peasantry obeyed the Persian aristocrats whose castles
dominated each wooded valley. This inner country contained
no cities, as a Greek understood the term; though there were
crowded villages, and a few immense royal fortresses. But by a
city a Greek did not mean a built-up area, however numerous
the population; municipal self-government was the essential
mark of civic status. Ten thousand serfs living under the walls
of a royal palace could make up nothing more than a large
village.

Instead of cities this inner land was centred on great temples.
These shrines must have been among the earliest institutions in
the country, venerated since the first neolithic farmers struggled
north over Taurus. To his worshippers the divinity in the
numinous place had no personal name; he was the godhead
who controlled everything. But of course inquiring Greeks must
give him a label, and for preference a name which equated him
with one of the denizens of Olympus. The most famous holy
place in northern Cappadocia was Amasia, on the upper Lycus.
Round the great shrine, and the mighty royal fortress, clustered
thousands of priests, temple-servants, and labourers who tilled
the land owned by the god. The figure venerated was that of an
armed male; he was known among the Greeks as Zeus Stratios.

The King spent most of his time at Amasia; therefore he

16

could control its high priest. But at Comana, the second holy place higher up the river, the high priest must be a trusted member of the royal family. In precedence he was the second dignitary of the Kingdom, coming immediately after the King. Six thousand serfs tilled the lands of his temple. The proprietor of this estate was a female figure, armed, who had no exact equivalent in the Olympic pantheon; therefore to men of every tongue she was known simply as Ma. It was fortunate that her name was easy to pronounce, for among her Cappadocian worshippers no less than twenty different tongues were spoken.

Such was northern Cappadocia, the true heart of Pontus; an ancient, fertile, rustic land, where farmers who were serfs but not slaves worked loyally for nobles whose high descent commanded universal veneration. It was a land of castles, and a land of horses; each noble castellan led a war-band of brave cavaliers.

Pontus proper, the southern shore of the Euxine, lay in a different world; the progressive, modern world of Hellenistic innovation. The free cities of Sinope and Amisus were proud of their Greek traditions. For centuries the Greek colonists of the Euxine had preserved their identity among surrounding hosts of barbarians; they were sailors rather than soldiers, self-reliant freemen well able to take care of themselves in any environment.

These Greek cities had been restive under Persian rule, and when Darius was overthrown by Alexander they snatched at independence. But in the wider Hellenistic world a single city could not stand alone. When even the Greek homeland was ruled by the King of Macedonia Sinope might without shame seek the protection of the King of Pontus. The cities managed their internal affairs, and in strict legal theory they were allies rather than subjects of the King; but their citadels held Pontic garrisons, and their ships served in the Pontic navy.

Thus Pontus stood slightly apart from the other Hellenistic Kingdoms, more truly Asiatic and less influenced by Greek culture. Socially, its monarch could be as Greek as any Ptolemy or as oriental as any Parthian; he was at home in two ways of life.

To complete the geographical setting we must mention Armenia, the highlands directly to the east of Pontus. Here was

B   17

Prologue

a completely oriental Kingdom of warlike mountaineers, scarcely known to the most adventurous Greek. Since it had a quarrelsome nobility and no undisputed royal line it was usually the scene of civil war. Its precarious King was an untrustworthy vassal of the Great King in Antioch; before this story opens it had barely impinged on the politics of the Mediterranean.

Under their splendid and useless Kings the Hellenistic realms had achieved a certain stability. Mercenary armies were perpetually on the march; but they did little harm, either to their foes or to the civil population. Even in time of war the frontiers remained open and trade moved freely. Asia Minor, prosperous and content, was well able to support half a dozen spendthrift dynasties.

Into this settled world, which bears some resemblance to eighteenth-century Europe, burst a nation of fierce soldiers who were also greedy money-grubbers. In the year 200 B.C. Rome, having defeated Carthage, invaded Macedonia; and about the same time Hannibal, the exiled Carthaginian leader, sought refuge from Roman revenge at the court of Antioch. In 192 Antiochus the Great, King of Kings, doing his duty as leader of Hellenism, marched to drive the Romans from Greece; he was speedily thrown out of Europe, and in 190 his forces were completely defeated at Magnesia in Asia Minor by the combined armies of Rome and Pergamum.

At first this appeared to mean no more than the addition of another power to what may be termed the Concert of the Hellenistic world. Pergamum extended her territories, and the Great King abandoned the fiction that every other ruler was rightfully his vassal. The Roman armies went home to Italy.

But Roman diplomatists remained behind to regulate the affairs of every state west of the Halys. To separate Bithynia from Pontus a weak and unviable Kingdom was set up in Paphlagonia; a confederation of tribal chiefs attempted to rule independent Galatia; Rhodes, already distinguished as the faithful ally of Rome, was granted the mainland territories of Lycia and southern Caria. The Roman envoys interfered in everything; especially they strove to get Hannibal, the famous exile, delivered to them. In this they were unsuccessful. Though the Great King drove him from Antioch he wandered among the other courts, until at last he cheated his unrelenting enemies by committing suicide at Nicomedia, while his host the King of Bithynia hesitated whether to betray him.

Hellenistic statesmen had never before dealt with anyone like these Roman envoys, and they could not begin to understand them. In four particulars Rome was quite unlike any other power of the second century. The first and most important was that the Roman army was the best in the world; it was quite certain that Rome would win any war in which she put forth all her strength. From that it followed that the commands of Rome must be obeyed. But the second point made things much more difficult. Greek ambassadors discovered to their surprise that Rome was genuinely an aristocratic republic, except for Rhodes the only republic in the civilized world. From time to time the Roman People met in their assembly to pass laws. But foreign affairs were directed by the Senate; that was a chamber of nobles with a fluctuating majority, which frequently changed its mind and reversed its policy. You might bribe or convince the Roman envoy at your court, but perhaps the treaty he had sealed would not be ratified by his city. If you sent an ambassador to Rome a particular Senator would be commissioned to negotiate with him; but he could not guarantee that the Senate as a whole would vote for the agreement he had concluded, and if your envoy reinsured by negotiating with the opposition he might be expelled with ignominy for interfering in the domestic politics of a friendly power. Nobody could discover what the Roman Republic really wanted.

The two remaining points added to the complications. It soon became clear that the Roman Senate as a corporate body did not wish to increase the extent of territory under its rule; already there were enough important posts overseas for everyone who mattered, and if more provinces were created they would have to be governed by new men, unworthy of a seat in the Senate. But each individual Roman envoy wished to make his name famous in the annals of his city by overthrowing a foreign King and adding to the dominions of his country.

Greek diplomatists, highly skilled in negotiating with their colleagues from other Kingdoms, could not cope with these queer barbarians from the west. The uncouth manners of the newcomers made it even more difficult; they spoke a tongue unknown in the civilized world, they were puffed up with pride, and they lacked courtesy. Matters came to a head in the year 168. Perseus, King of Macedonia, was badgered into declaring war on Rome; he was quickly conquered. Macedonia was one of the great powers of the Hellenistic world, in fact the power which had brought that world into being; now the Kingdom vanished, split into petty chieftaincies. In the autumn of the same year Antiochus Epiphanes, King of Kings, was marching to the invasion of Egypt when he encountered a Roman envoy. Rome had guaranteed Egyptian integrity, and Popilius Laenas ordered him to halt. The Great King offered to summon his councillors, and with their advice compose a fitting answer to the Senate. With the end of his herald's staff Popilius drew a circle round the King's feet; before he left this circle Antiochus must agree to obey the commands of Rome, or face all-out war.

Antiochus yielded, in fear of the Roman armies. This famous interview increased the prestige of Rome as a military power, but it displayed also the bad manners of her diplomatists.

From long habit both Greeks and Romans thought of the King of Kings as a mighty potentate, though in fact by the second century Syria was no longer a strong military power. The Romans set themselves to stir up the enemies of a country they considered dangerous, until about the year 150 Syria collapsed. The Parthians advanced to the left bank of the Euphrates, and the rest of the Levant broke up into a mosaic of petty states.

From the Nile to the Hellespont the Romans had upset the balance of power, pulling down one after another every ruler who promised to found a strong administration. Yet Rome would not step in to take over the vacant hegemony. King Eumenes of Pergamum decided to preserve his Kingdom by acting throughout his reign as the faithful ally, some said the jackal, of Rome. For a time Rome encouraged him to extend his boundaries; then presently the Senate grew jealous of the increase of his power, and began to support his rival and neighbour, the King of Bithynia. The friends of Rome enjoyed no more security than her enemies.

The situation was intolerable, as eventually became clear even to one party among the Romans. Either Rome must get out of the East, or she must govern there. At last the advocates of a forward policy gained control of the Senate, and in 148 Macedonia was declared to be an ordinary Roman province. This stirred the Achaean League in Greece proper to attack their overbearing protectors. The result was the conquest of Greece. Famous cities were indeed still permitted to call themselves independent; the proudest Roman did not deem himself worthy to be military governor of Athens or Sparta. But any alliance between cities was forbidden, and the few Greek states which had retained any military resources were ordered to disarm. The ancient world acknowledged a truism which we have forgotten, that democracy is always more bellicose than the rule of the gentry. Throughout the Greek cities Rome abolished popular government, and installed in its place oligarchic corporations.

Perhaps Hellenistic statesmen on the far side of the Aegean did not greatly mourn the downfall of Greece. Those decaying little towns had been the scene of some dangerous social experiments, as bankrupt party-leaders clung to power by cancelling debts or freeing the slaves of their opponents. They could fulfil their functions as museums of architecture or seats of higher education just as well under the protection of Roman arms. But everyone was shocked at the downfall of Corinth.

That wealthy commercial and manufacturing city had been in the forefront of resistance to Rome, and had surrendered only after a bitter siege. The Roman army sacked it thoroughly, burned every house in the town, and sold into slavery all the inhabitants, male and female. For a hundred years the site of Corinth lay desolate.

Such an atrocity was clean outside the tradition of Hellenistic warfare. Two hundred years ago King Philip, father of Alexander the Great, had destroyed the city of Thebes; that was still remembered with abhorrence, as the greatest blot on his reputation. Of recent years a genuine Greek city had come to be regarded as something sacred; the successors of Alexander boasted of the cities they founded, not of the cities they destroyed. These Romans were really intolerable.

The Romans had another intolerable vice, their disgusting cruelty to slaves. Slavery was widespread throughout the ancient world, because it was generally believed that civilization could not exist without it. But Greek tradition was on the whole kindly to slaves. No distinction of colour, no great distinction of language or manners, marked off the free citizen from the slave who waited on him. Labour in the mines was notoriously unhealthy, and slaves condemned to it quickly died of disease; but as far as possible these were criminals sent underground as a punishment. Many household slaves were really household pets, skilled craftsmen were carefully cherished, and among the labourers on a farm a stranger could hardly distinguish the slaves from free wage-earners. Especially in Asia great estates were worked by whole communities of serfs rather than true slaves. Each ploughman lived in his own cottage, with his own wife and children. He worked hard, and got nothing for it but his keep; but in general his lot was little harder than that of the free peasant who tills the same fields at the present day.

That was not the Roman attitude to slavery. The Romans were a brave people, who themselves, when misfortune struck, faced pain and death without repining. But in their eyes non-Romans had very few rights, and men who had accepted slavery instead of death merited no consideration at all. When they suddenly found themselves very wealthy they decided that the slaughter of valuable slaves was an agreeable method of displaying their riches. The horrors of the amphitheatre were shocking to every Greek; to make men fight wild animals, and then arrange that the men should be beaten, was in Greek eyes a treacherous betrayal of human dignity. To use men, even slaves, just as things diminished the honour of Man as a species.

The Romans took pleasure in cruelty; Greeks recognized that pleasure could be found there, but they considered such pleasure too degrading for the enjoyment of rational beings. Roman ruthlessness was even more disgusting than Roman cruelty. A Roman master screwed the last ounce of work out of his slaves, and treated them with less consideration than he would have shown to a good horse. The great estates of Italy possessed no villages where serfs might live a family life. The labourers, all men, were locked up every night in communal dungeons; the old and the sick were thrown out to starve.

Within the sphere of Roman influence the slave trade was more active than in Hellenistic lands. The high priests of

Prologue

Comana and Amasia were forbidden to sell their temple-serfs; but Rome imposed tribute, and Roman officials demanded bribes. Nobles who had in the past exacted nothing but labour from their unfree villagers were now compelled to part with labourers for ready cash; the island of Delos, the central market of this traffic, had in the second century an enormous annual turnover. A slave sold from Asia into Italy found his lot changed immeasurably for the worse.

The result of this oppression was servile revolt, which previously had not troubled the Mediterranean world. In 134 the slaves of Sicily rebelled, and formed themselves into an army which conquered the whole interior of the island. Their suppression entailed a war of four years which engaged the whole Roman army, led by the Consuls who were the highest Roman commanders-in-chief.

About this time a new sect of philosophers began to preach the universal brotherhood of man with more earnestness than their predecessors, though this belief had always been a commonplace of Greek philosophy. The slaves of Asia Minor learned that they had been robbed of their birthright, and educated men were willing to lead them. The Kings were perpetually badgered by the Roman Senate, which, yet when it came to the point, would not send an army to preserve order; their nobles were forced to raise large sums in ready cash to placate Roman envoys; the slaves, on whose labour rested the whole fabric of civilization, were on the brink of revolt; and the Romans as individuals were disliked as much as they were feared. From the Aegean to the Caucasus trouble was brewing.

While this unrest was at its height the Roman Republic for the first time extended its boundaries into Asia. King Attalus III of Pergamum died in the year 133, bequeathing his dominions to the Roman People. After some hesitation the Senate accepted the bequest. The Greek cities on the coast of Pergamum were left in nominal freedom, but the inland districts became the Roman province of Asia. It was to be governed directly by a Roman proconsul, the elected magistrate who had just finished his year of office as Consul. This proconsul would come out for one year of governorship, ignorant of the language and customs of his new subjects; he would expect to make his fortune during his term of office, and he would be accompanied

---

Prologue

by a crowd of hungry hangers-on; the only appeal from his decisions would lie to the Senate, made up of his friends and relations who themselves hoped to be one day proconsul of Asia. It was about the worst form of government that the mind of man could devise.

What impelled King Attalus to make this disastrous disposition of his Kingdom remains a mystery. Probably one factor was a desire for a secure old age. The normal end of a Hellenistic King was to be murdered by his heir; after the terms of his will were known no one would have any incentive to poison Attalus. But perhaps, in despair, he thought it was the best thing he could do for his people. The Romans already interfered in every branch of his government; let them have responsibility as well as power, and perhaps they would consider the welfare of the Pergamenes.

The Greek coastal cities felt that they could manage their new masters as easily as they had managed the Kings; they acquiesced in the change, and at first welcomed the Italian settlers who brought the promise of increased trade with the west. But the serfs of the countryside, in fear of the slave-dealers of Delos, at once rose in insurrection.

A group of nobles, seeing that their importance would vanish with the court, put themselves at the head of the revolt. They proclaimed Aristonicus, half-brother of the late Attalus, as the next King of independent Pergamum. The strange alliance of aristocrats and serfs was supported by the new philosophical sect, the Heliopolitae, whose membership extended even to Rome. King Aristonicus maintained himself in inner Pergamum, while Roman armies held the coast. The war continued for several years, and in 130 a Roman proconsul was killed in battle at the head of his men. If the neighbouring Kingdoms had made common cause with the rebels the Romans might have been driven finally from the east.

But Hellenistic Kingdoms were always eager to prey on one another. The Romans offered the bait of the dismemberment of Pergamum, and the other Kings marched eagerly to invasion and plunder. In 128 Aristonicus was overthrown. The greater part of Pergamum became the new Roman province of Asia, while Pontus and Cappadocia were rewarded respectively with the Pergamene territories of Phrygia and Lycaonia. In

24

Prologue

Sicily the slave-revolt had been put down, and throughout the extended Roman dominions there prevailed an uneasy peace.

At the height of these troubles, in the autumn of the year 132, a son was born to Laodice, Queen of King Mithradates V of Pontus. The child was named Mithradates after his father.

I

The King of Pontus

Young Mithradates was the eldest son of King Mithradates V, and of Laodice his Queen; who had already borne a daughter, and in the next few years presented her husband with a second son and four more girls. Dynastic pride made a thorough muddle of the naming of these children. The Queen was a Seleucid from Antioch, so this noble connexion must be perpetuated in her daughters; the two elder girls were both called Laodice. The younger daughters were given Persian names, Roxana, Statira, Nysa, to remind the world that Achaemenid blood flowed in their veins. In the same way, both sons of King Mithradates V must be named after him. But Kings and their sons did something to clear up the confusion thus inflicted on chroniclers and genealogists. At that time Kings of the same name were not distinguished by a number, but by nicknames. Yet the example of the French Carolingians, Charles the Bald and Charles the Fat, shows that nicknames bestowed by public opinion are not always complimentary. Prudently, Hellenistic rulers chose their own adjectives. Mithradates V called himself Euergetes, the Benefactor; his elder son was Mithradates Eupator, the Good Father, and his second Mithradates Chrestus, the Virtuous. These second names appear officially on coins and documents, and enable us to tell apart at least the male members of the family.

Mithradates Eupator was born in the royal palace at Sinope, the Greek seaport that was the usual residence of Mithradates Euergetes. There he passed his childhood, and in consequence he was brought up as a Greek; the sons of prominent Greek citizens were his companions, sharing his lessons and his amusements. In later life his most intimate friends and the women he loved were Greeks; and, though he understood more than a score

26

of languages, Greek seems to have been the tongue he spoke for preference.

But he never forgot that he was by descent an Achaemenid, a royal Persian. Even at Greek banquets, even when offering at Greek shrines, he wore the traditional dress of a Persian noble: a sleeved tunic and baggy trousers caught at the ankle. In his embroidered belt he carried a jewel-hilted dagger.

This proves that he did not mind being stared at; for such a costume would look as odd in a Greek city as a Red Indian war-bonnet in London. It would also carry the same connotation of savagery. As outer garments Greeks wore long gowns, which left their arms bare; they had a particular aversion to any form of trouser, which they considered ridiculously barbarous. To carry a weapon openly within the walls of a city was even more barbarous than to wear trousers.

Strange stories were told about the self-willed boy who walked through Sinope in such unseemly garb. Someone who behaved so oddly must be destined for great things. It was rumoured that his birth had coincided with the first appearance of a remarkable comet, whose radiance filled a quarter of the heavens and for a few days even outshone the sun. There must be an omen in that, though the full explanation did not become clear until Mithradates was dead. The second rumour was even more ominous. It was said that lightning had played about the infant's cradle, and that he had taken no hurt from it; even though the bolt from heaven had actually touched his brow, where it left a scar in the shape of a diadem. The gods themselves had marked him out to be a mighty ruler.

Meanwhile Mithradates Euergetes, father of the young prince, was cautiously increasing his power; though he never overstepped the narrow bounds of action permitted to a King who wished to keep the friendship of Rome. A timely loan of his fleet, manned by the excellent Greek sailors of the Pontic sea-board, gained him the important title of 'Friend and Ally of the Roman People'. At the dismemberment of the Kingdom of Pergamum he bought from the Roman commissioner, Manius Aquilius, the Pergamene district of Phrygia. The grant was never ratified by the Senate; and in after years the proconsul in Roman Asia claimed Phrygia as part of his governorship. But the well-trained mercenaries of Pontus garrisoned the land, and during his brief period of office each Roman proconsul in turn could be bribed not to press his claim to the point of hostilities. Phrygia remained in Pontic occupation.

Then the King of Paphlagonia, dying without heirs, bequeathed his tiny realm to his neighbour of Pontus. Again the Roman Senate did not ratify the change of boundaries; but again the Pontic army moved forward, until Pontus stood once more on the frontier of Bithynia. The chieftains of lawless Galatia greedily accepted Pontic bribes, and in return acknowledged Pontus as their suzereign. A mercenary general in Pontic employment, one Dorylaus, intervened in the unending wars between the little pirate-cities of Crete. To annex that island to Pontus would mean an open breach with Rome; but friendly pirates might come in handy one day.

Mithradates Euergetes achieved his boldest triumph in foreign policy when he married his eldest daughter to young King Ariarathes of Cappadocia. At the time of the wedding the bridegroom was still too young to rule in person, and his mother as regent governed the Kingdom. A Pontic princess would not take kindly to the rule of her mother-in-law; and recent precedent seemed to promise misfortune for the boy-King. The last Queen-regent of Cappadocia, Nysa by name, had retained power by the expedient of murdering her five sons, one after the other, as they approached the age when they would displace her. Laodice of Pontus was taking no chances; she persuaded her young husband to murder his mother before she murdered him. Thus Cappadocia became in practice a dependency of Pontus.

It seemed to some onlookers that Mithradates Euergetes was strengthening his realm with the object of one day breaking free from Roman tutelage. He had not reckoned with his Queen. This eldest Laodice was probably the daughter of Antiochus Epiphanes, the King of Syria who had been so grossly humiliated by Popilius Laenas. She had very good reason to fear the Romans, and she was determined to end her days as a crowned Queen, not as a trophy in some Roman triumph. Accordingly, no one in Pontus was particularly surprised when one day in the year 120 King Mithradates Euergetes was assassinated by his courtiers in his palace at Sinope. As soon as he was dead a will was produced, by whose terms it was alleged that he had

28

left his Kingdom jointly to his two sons, with their mother as regent until they were old enough to rule in person. That time was fairly distant, for Mithradates Eupator was then in his twelfth year, and Chrestus younger.

When Queen Laodice was in command the foreign policy of Pontus was put into reverse. In the palace at Sinope a Queen-regent could lead a very happy life, and the revenues of Pontus in its narrowest sense would be ample for her support. But the key to a pleasant and peaceful old age was the friendship of Rome, and that could be earned only by complete obscurity and a withdrawal from foreign adventure. The Pontic army retired from Phrygia and Paphlagonia, the Galatian chieftains were advised to obey the orders of the Roman proconsul, and in Crete Dorylaus was disavowed by the widow of his previous employer; his forces continued in the field, but henceforth they were paid by Cretan cities. Queen Laodice of Cappadocia, who held real power in the name of her feckless husband, was advised by her mother, Queen Laodice of Pontus, to seek the friendship of the Roman authorities in Pergamum. As a whole this made up a coherent policy of voluntary servitude, similar to that followed by certain native rulers in nineteenth-century India; who knew that British power was too strong to be withstood, but that ample revenues and an undisturbed private life could be secured by unquestioning loyalty to the British Viceroy.

But if the Queen of Pontus reduced her military forces and spent the taxes of her small Kingdom on royal ceremonial in Sinope, the position she would leave to her sons when they came of age would be no more than that of wealthy but powerless subjects of Rome. Even if no Roman general presently confiscated their estates to pay his men, the two brothers would have dwindled very far from the mighty position of their ancestors. Young Mithradates Eupator saw with dismay the shrinking of his inheritance.

An even more awkward problem presently began to disturb him. If all went smoothly his mother was due to retire in his favour when he attained full age; as time went on it seemed more and more likely that he would suffer a fatal accident before that date. Sometimes he noticed a queer taste in his food. He knew what to do about that. It would appear that at the

The King of Pontus

Pontic court murder by slow poison had become such a matter of routine that it always followed the same course; one particular poison was employed in small cumulative doses, which were guaranteed to bring death with all the symptoms of natural disease. Some doctors believed they had discovered an antidote to this poison. Of this antidote the young man took a regular daily dose, a régime which he continued until the day of his death; he swallowed immediately afterwards a small dose of poison, to make sure that the antidote had been properly compounded. Soon he found that he could eat without ill effects the most elaborate confections of the palace cooks.

There still remained the chance of death by misadventure. The chase was his favourite amusement; but when he went hunting with his mother's friends stray arrows were always whizzing past his ear. His mother's grooms were even more incompetent; time and again they mounted him on some notorious man-killing stallion. Even as a boy he was noted for his magnificent horsemanship. Each time he subdued the savage bolter or buckjumper, and came home safely. But any pitcher can go too often to the well. Young Mithradates Eupator grew tired of narrow escapes.

 About the time of his fourteenth birthday, therefore, that is to say in the autumn of 118, he set off on a hunting trip with a small party of young friends whom he could really trust. The expedition carried supplies for several days. The plan was that they should ride through the wooded hills of inland Pontus, hunting by day and by night camping out in tents.

Weeks passed, and then months; the young prince and his trusted friends did not return to Sinope. Nobles of ancient Persian stock, ruling their secluded fiefs from craggy castles deep in the forest, welcomed their young chieftain whenever he chose to call. These nobles cared nothing for the Greek Queen-regent who lived down on the coast among those foreign Greek citizens; and so long as they sent their full tribute the Queen-regent cared nothing for them. Nevertheless, young Mithradates did not relax his precautions. He took his daily dose of the antidote, and to make doubly sure he ate only game which had fallen to his own arrow. He visited the castles of his vassals for an occasional bath and haircut, and presumably to replace foundered horses and worn-out clothes. Sometimes he would stay for dinner, if he trusted his host. But every night he slept in the forest, through summer heat or winter snow. His tent was moved every day, and no one knew in advance where it would be pitched.

For seven years he lived like Robin Hood in the greenwood, though he was rightful King over every valley in which he hunted. The life suited him. He grew up tall and strong and handsome, the best horseman in Asia, famous for his prowess with bow and javelin. To the nobles who rarely saw him, themselves descended from mighty horsemen who long ago had ridden westwards from Iran, he seemed the reincarnation of their heroic ancestors. Here was a leader worthy of the allegiance of well-born cavaliers, a better leader than that Greek woman who lolled on the hot and foreign coast.

Queen Laodice had given evidence of some efficiency in the daily round of Hellenistic statecraft; she had disposed of her husband neatly. But she was not really in the first class as a politician, for she did not keep her attention always at full stretch. When young Mithradates was out of sight she forgot about him. She may have regretted the need to murder her elder son in order to keep her throne; that he should disappear of his own volition was in every way a better solution. Little Chrestus might continue to live, for when that weakling was on the throne she would still be the real governor of the Kingdom. She was undisputed Queen of the only part of Pontus that mattered to her, the fringe of Greek cities scattered along the coast. Her elder son, lurking in the forest, might gather a few barbarous followers; but he could never overthrow her.

During the seven years of her son's exile Queen Laodice, a true Seleucid, occupied herself with the foundation of a new capital, the city of Laodicea on the shore of Lake Stiphanis. It was a city completely Greek, in which a native of Antioch might feel at home. Meanwhile her Roman overlords approved of her peaceful rule, the Pontic armed forces grew smaller every year, and the revenues were spent on courtly splendour. She seemed to be assured of a long and prosperous reign.

Suddenly, on a spring day in the year 111, a disturbance broke out in the city of Sinope. A youth whose beauty seemed rather divine than human appeared in the market-place, attired in splendid Persian trousers and mounted on a fiery steed. He proclaimed to the astonished citizens that he was their rightful King, compelled for many years to live in hiding to escape the dastardly plots of the Queen-regent.

A Greek crowd was easily swayed by male beauty. Even in his twenty-first year young Mithradates was a skilled orator. To idlers bored by the peaceful reign of the pro-Roman Queen he promised glory and the stir of action. Soon the able-bodied mob of Sinope fell in behind the young hero. He led them against the half-built city of Laodicea.

The Queen had no army, because she trusted in Roman protection. But there were no Roman troops nearer than Pergamum; and anyway, why should a Roman proconsul concern himself with yet another of the incessant palace revolutions which every year swept through one or another of these Hellenistic client-states? With the mob at her gates Laodice surrendered at discretion, hoping that when she was thus publicly his prisoner the new King would hesitate to incur the dreadful guilt of matricide. After such a notorious turmoil there could be no question of making away with her in secret.

Queen Laodice had decided wisely. Her victorious son showed himself merciful. The revolution went through without a check, and there were no executions. Young Mithradates even agreed to share his throne with Chrestus, in accordance with the terms of his father's alleged will; the names of the two rulers appear side by side on the coins of the new reign. Of course the Queen-mother was placed under arrest, never again to be seen in public. But that was a very much better fate than the end she had arranged for her husband. She did not long survive her loss of power, but it seems certain that she died in the ordinary course of nature. In later years many grave accusations were made against her elder son; but no one ever reproached him with the killing of his mother.

Young Chrestus was more of a problem. So long as he remained in the background he was merely an extra drain on the privy purse; but of course every disappointed courtier intrigued to make him the figurehead of another revolution. Within a few months he was arrested, tried publicly on a charge of plotting the assassination of his elder brother, and publicly executed. The accusation may well have been true. If he did not himself plot, others plotted on his behalf; the execution was generally

recognized to be just. By his twenty-first birthday young Mithradates was sole King of Pontus.

There was another bit of family business to be cleared up
before the young King could turn to affairs of state. He must
beget legitimate sons, to ensure the succession. His predecessors
had married princesses of predominantly Greek blood, but
young Mithradates had strong reasons for breaking with precedent. In the first place it was his policy to emphasize the native
Persian side of his mixed inheritance; he was heir to a cadet of
the Achaemenid line, not to a Macedonian general of division.
In the second place there was nowadays no Greek royal house
whose daughters were worthy to mate with Pontus. Pergamum
and Paphlagonia had vanished; Syria was falling into anarchy
as Arab tribal chiefs took over every prosperous city beyond the
gates of Antioch; Bithynia, Cappadocia, even Egypt, were now
mere Roman protectorates, preserving a nominal independence
as meaningless as the nominal independence of Athens or
Argos. The young King decided to make a new departure, for
which precedent could be found in the royal house of Egypt.
He married the younger of his two sisters Laodice (the elder
being already married to the King of Cappadocia).

The theory behind a union of this kind was well known to the
ancients: the royal line of Pontus was so distinguished that no
other family in the world was worthy to marry with it. Oddly
enough, though incest committed by private individuals was
reprobated with superstitious horror as likely to bring down on
the whole community the vengeance of heaven, these incestuous
royal marriages incurred no popular reproach. Kings are not
of the same kind as ordinary men, and they should be judged
by different rules.

Young Mithradates was both logical and careful. If only his
sister was worthy to be his Queen, and if by custom he could
have only one Queen at a time, then no husband was available
for his other sisters. Besides, he must have sons. Laodice might
prove barren, or she might die young. His three younger sisters
were confined in unmarried seclusion. Save for a few virgin
priestesses, spinsters were unknown in antiquity. This treatment of his sisters was considered one of the young King's
eccentricities. Another was his habit of carrying a sword always,
and at meals hanging up his bow and quiver where he could

c

The King of Pontus

reach them; but that could be explained by the experiences of his youth.

Unnoticed by his subjects, he was already doing something very remarkable. At the age of 21, an absolute ruler surrounded by flatterers, he had embarked with caution on a long-term policy which would show results only after many years. He was determined that Pontus should be an independent power, not a Roman satellite; but he knew that any open display of vigour and ability would bring down on him the invincible legions. He must enlarge and safeguard his frontiers. But it was vital that the Roman proconsul in Pergamum should not notice what he was doing.

His mother had left him no armed forces at all. He began modestly by hiring a band of 6,000 Greek mercenaries. That could not frighten anybody; in numbers it was the equivalent of one Roman legion, and in military value very much inferior.

It was difficult to find a field of action for these soldiers. He was the ally of Rome, bound by treaty not to make war on any other state allied to her. On his eastern frontier, where he could look beyond the Roman sphere of influence, Armenia was becoming a great power, too strong to be invaded from mere lust of conquest.

Perhaps something could be done in Cappadocia, where a great nobleman named Gordius was his faithful friend. With lavish subsidies from the Pontic treasury Gordius raised a rebel army, and the wretched King Ariarathes was defeated and slain.

Thenceforth Cappadocia was ruled *de jure* by Mithradates' sister Laodice the elder, as regent for her son Ariarathes VII; but in fact the government was in the hands of Gordius, the obedient servant of Mithradates. In spite of their kinship Queen Laodice never supported her brother; she agreed with her late mother's opinion that real power had passed to Rome, and that the safest way to enjoy its trappings was to be the faithful ally of the Roman People. In addition she had loved her mother, and detested the brother who had imprisoned her. But while Gordius was her minister she must obey Pontus.

Within a year of his accession Mithradates had secured his southern frontier. He could not expand to the west, where Rome guaranteed the safety of her clients; or to the east, where Armenia was growing as the strength of Syria waned. With the

34

The King of Pontus

Euxine as his northern boundary Pontus seemed to be encircled.

But the Greek cities on his coast gave him an efficient navy, save for a small Bithynian squadron the only navy in the Euxine. In all her long history Rome never produced a competent admiral, or even a warship manned by a native Roman crew. But at that time there was not so much as a permanent squadron of warships, even manned by Greek mercenaries, flying the Roman flag anywhere in the Mediterranean. Pontus dominated the Euxine.

Civilized Greek soldiers would find a welcome on its northern shore; for in the Crimea and the opposite Kertch Peninsula remote Greek cities were oppressed by barbarian neighbours. Of these cities Panticapaeum was the chief. It was a genuinely Greek town, as were the other lesser settlements; but they lay very far from the main stream of Greek life.

These Greek colonies were essential to the economy of the Aegean. For more than three hundred years Athens had depended on annual imports of wheat from what is now southern Russia. The Greek settlers farmed extensive cornlands of their own, and they bought with the wine and olive oil of Europe even greater quantities of grain from the barbarians. But to Greek eyes the Pontic Chersonese was very far away at the back of beyond, and growing wheat was not the way to make a fortune. The cities of the Chersonese never grew strong enough to stand on their own feet. At first the settlers paid tribute to the barbarians; but as soon as they had bought the goodwill of one tribe of Scythians another tribe would overthrow it and demand a second tribute. In the second century B.C. the Greeks tried the desperate expedient of calling in barbarian chieftains to rule them; but the particular barbarian they picked was never strong enough, so that in addition to supporting an expensive autocrat they still had to pay blackmail to their neighbours. Now at last one party in the cities was looking for a foreign protector. An embassy appealed to the King of Pontus; and a Pontic army sailed to their assistance.

This decision to expand northwards was the first sign that Mithradates was no ordinary man. No earlier ruler of Pontus had seen the Euxine as anything but a barrier; once the idea had lodged in his mind it seemed as obvious as Columbus's

35

method of standing an egg on its end. It could offend nobody. Though the Chersonese is joined to the mainland of Europe, at that time it was for practical purposes an island. The swampy mouths of the Danube barred the overland route from Thrace, and the alternative road round the eastern end of the Euxine was cut by the savages of the Caucasus. The Romans were not interested in what happened to a small district many days' sail from the eastern limit of their dominions. If they took note of what was going on in this remote corner of civilization, they could only be grateful that a Greek-speaking King had undertaken the public duty of defending helpless Greeks from barbarians.

The Pontic forces had some stiff fighting before the Chersonese was reduced to obedience. The Scythians naturally resisted this foreign invasion, and one faction among the Greek settlers would rather pay tribute to barbarians outside the city than admit the troops of an absolute King within their walls. But by the year 106 the Crimea and the opposite shore of the Sea of Azov had been organized into the Kingdom of Bosporus (the classical name for the Straits of Kertch), with Mithradates of Pontus as King.

In the same year Mithradates received the allegiance of Colchis, a small barbarian trading post at the eastern end of the Euxine. It took three campaigns to make this allegiance a reality, but afterwards the Colchians proved loyal subjects. Their land was proverbially at the edge of the known world, the far-off magic region whence Jason had fetched Medea and the Golden Fleece; but its people had always been eager for trade with the west, and they were pleased to be drawn closer into the comity of nations.

That comity of nations, the trading world of the Mediterranean, was now united under the hegemony of Rome. In the beginning the sea-faring culture of Hellas had been confined to the Aegean; under Alexander it had expanded to embrace the Levant and much of the Euxine; the rise of Carthage and then of Rome had joined to it the Tyrrhenian Sea as far as the Pillars of Hercules. All the basin of the Mediterranean was now a unity, from Gades to Colchis; the trade-routes radiating from Rome brought to Asia speedy news of every happening on its shores.

The King of Pontus

In the year 105 news drifted eastward of a great battle in southern Gaul. That news would bring a thrill of anxiety mingled with hope to every market-place where Greeks lived behind stone walls. Very far away, on the foggy borders of the Celtic west, a Roman army had been destroyed by a new race of savages. The appearance of the great host of Cimbri and Teutones was the first contact between Germans and the civilized world. That Roman defeat at Arausio (Orange) would be discussed in every gathering of subject Greeks, as half a century ago the defeat of imperial Russia by Japan was discussed in every Asiatic bazaar. Rome was not invincible. Perhaps the days of freedom would return.

By this time Mithradates Eupator was in truth King of Pontus, King of every civilized harbour in the Euxine. He had a small army of trained Greek mercenaries, and a fleet manned by excellent Greek sailors. From among his native subjects in upland Cappadocia he could recruit thousands of good horsemen. He was on friendly terms with the Scythians of the steppe, who were accustomed to enlisting under foreign rulers. At short notice he could raise as many troops, good troops, as he could pay. Rather surprisingly, he had plenty of money with which to pay them.

How Mithradates became so rich remains a mystery. Every Asiatic ruler stored up treasure, against the sudden crisis when he must hire mercenaries or lose his throne. But Romans had an exaggerated idea of the fabled wealth of the orient, and the bribes which each annual proconsul of Asia annually exacted were draining the silver of Asia into Rome. We know that the King of Cappadocia was normally insolvent, the Galatian chieftains penniless, and even the favoured King of Bithynia hard pressed for ready cash. Mithradates could always draw on a full treasury. Perhaps the extension of his dominions, to form a single trading area embracing all the shores of the Euxine, gave him a great revenue from commercial dues; perhaps the rise of Parthia had shifted the terminus of the overland Chinese silk-route from the Euphrates to Colchis; perhaps he merely kept good peace in a naturally rich land. Whatever the explanation, he was never short of money.

It cannot be a coincidence that 104, the year in which the main Roman armies were hard pressed in southern Gaul, was

37

The King of Pontus

also the year when the Kings of Pontus and Bithynia formed an alliance which they must have known would displease their Roman masters. The object of the alliance was the joint plunder of the lesser states on their borders. First their combined armies overran Paphlagonia and Galatia. Having thus secured his western and southern borders, Mithradates then sent his forces eastward. The Kingdom of Armenia was too strong to be provoked; but west of the Euphrates lay a turbulent district known as Lesser Armenia, whose numerous castellans acknowledged no superior lord. Soon the Pontic army had reduced this land to order, and by a solemn treaty the King of Armenia fixed his frontier with Pontus on the river Euphrates.

But in 102 the Roman general Marius utterly defeated the German invaders. After all, Rome was supreme. Little Kings in Asia must tread warily.

In January 100 the King of Pontus, Bosporus, and Colchis was 31 years of age, tall, handsome, vigorous, the most powerful ruler in Asia. He was intelligent, a patron of letters who got on well with his Greek subjects, a mighty sportsman and athlete who had won the admiration of the native aristocracy. He was a promising young man. But as yet he had done nothing remarkable, save to pick skilful mercenary captains and get good results from them; and it so happened that he had never travelled beyond the boundary of his native land. Now he thought it safe to leave his Kingdom (always a perilous business for an autocrat) to improve his education by the Grand Tour.

During his absence his Queen and sister Laodice would govern, with the advice of a council of the King's Friends. King's Friend was an official rank, the highest official rank in Pontus, though it was open to men of every class in society. Mithradates travelled incognito. But this was only to avoid tiresome official receptions; he made no effort to conceal his identity, and in fact wore his Persian trousers even in Greek cities where they were a rare sight. To mark his visit to the famous shrine of Apollo at Delos he erected votive tablets bearing his name and the names of his companions, tablets which have survived to our own day.

Delos was his farthest port of call, which shows that the object of his tour was not sightseeing but the gathering of political information; otherwise surely he would have continued to the mainland of Greece. Delos was then the greatest trading port in the Aegean, a convenient centre in which to learn the news of the world.

His tour began with a visit to the Roman province of Asia, which had once been the Kingdom of Pergamum. He would note that it was very badly governed, grossly overtaxed and in great disorder. Roman rule was unpopular, and if they received help from outside the Pergamenes would be glad to revolt.

Farther on, the republic of Rhodes was the only Greek city-state still enjoying genuine independence, with its own militia and a regular navy. Such a city might one day be a useful ally. The King of Pontus celebrated his visit with such munificent gifts for public purposes that in return the grateful Rhodians erected a statue of him in their market-place.

He touched at two other nominally independent Greek cities, Heraclea and Cyzicus. They were permitted to manage their internal affairs; but they would not dare to dispute even un-lawful orders from a Roman magistrate. Although these cities had now no military force their walls were kept in repair and they were strong fortresses.

Bithynia was a civilized Greek Kingdom, well governed and prosperous. Its King, Nicomedes II, was an ally of the Romans. But he was their friend of his own free will, because he thought their friendship worth having; not a mere subject honoured with nominal independence. He paid a small but efficient army, and an even smaller navy. Bithynia was a puny power, but among the Kingdoms of Asia it came second only to Pontus.

Paphlagonia was a mosaic of tiny baronies, ruled either by chiefs of aboriginal stock or by immigrant Galatian freebooters. But then in the view of the ancient world everything Paphla-gonian was slightly ridiculous; on the comic stage a Paphla-gonian slave was the typical country bumpkin.

Galatia was another Paphlagonia, not quite so comic because it was even more barbarous. Neither of these countries could matter politically, except as possible theatres of war.

In Cappadocia the Queen-regent was his sister Laodice the elder, who disliked him. But Cappadocia was utterly bankrupt, ravaged from end to end by pirates and slave-raiders. Since a penniless Queen was powerless for good or evil there was no point in trying to regain the affection of his sister.

The King of Pontus

A small Roman garrison occupied Cilicia, under the command of a propraetor. His position was anomalous, for in law Cilicia was not Roman territory. The propraetor's 'province', i.e. his official duty, was the command of a Roman army of occupation on foreign soil. The garrison was there to keep an eye on the Great King in Antioch; for Cilicia, bounded on the north by the steep range of Taurus, communicates more easily with Syria than with the plateau of Asia Minor.

It was not the duty of the propraetor to govern Cilicia, yet his mere presence made it impossible for anyone else to govern there. The rugged coast was broken by excellent harbours; though few Greek cities had been founded beside them because of the poverty of the rocky soil. In the breakdown of order which followed the expulsion of the Great King these harbours had been appropriated by a new power, just emerging on the political scene: the pirates who had always infested the Mediterranean were now building forts at the head of these narrow fiords, castles which could house safely their women and their plunder. Now that they had found a secure base the pirates naturally coalesced into larger squadrons; their united fleets not only snapped up stray merchant ships but besieged and carried by assault walled cities.

This was a direct though unintended result of Roman policy. The suppression of piracy had in the past been the duty of the strongest naval power in the Levant; long ago Athens had undertaken it, then the Ptolemies of Egypt, and latterly the republic of Rhodes. But the Romans, who would not build a navy for themselves, were jealous of other fleets; Rhodes and Bithynia were compelled by treaty to limit the numbers of their warships, and at the annexation of Pergamum the Pergamene navy was disbanded. There was left no sea power strong enough to police the Levant; the pirates, unmolested on deep water, could combine to raid the land.

A generation ago Mithradates Euergetes, intervening in the civil wars of Crete, had entered into close relations with these pirates, who then controlled many Cretan cities. After Crete had been attacked by the Roman general Antonius the pirates prudently moved farther east. It seems reasonable to suppose, though no record of it has come down to us, that during his tour of Cilicia Mithradates Eupator got in touch with these old friends of his father, who later served him faithfully. He may well have been the first statesman to observe that a new force had arisen south of Taurus, while the attention of every other onlooker was concentrated on the break-up of the Seleucid Empire.

Mithradates was an intelligent man, who for more than ten years had been ruling a prosperous and growing Kingdom. His tour of the neighbouring states must have led him to some such conclusions as these:

Rome ruled supreme from Italy to the Euphrates; but her rule was based on prestige alone. Cilicia was held by one Roman legion, and there was a second in the province of Asia, making less than 12,000 regular foot in all. Their nearest supports were in Macedonia, whose garrison was fully occupied in holding the northern frontier against the barbarians of Thrace. Greece proper contained no Roman troops at all. If the proconsul of Asia needed reinforcements they must come by sea from beyond the Adriatic, and there was no Roman fleet to protect the convoy. In the eastern provinces Roman officials were accustomed to raise local levies to deal with any sudden emergency; but these local troops served them only from fear. Every Asiatic hated Roman rule, and so did most Greeks. What would happen if the main Roman army were fully engaged in some other theatre? A revolt that defeated the two legions in Asia would bring over all the time-servers who hated their masters as much as they feared them. The plan was already forming in his mind. As soon as a great war should provide the opportunity he would put it into effect.

But his first business when he returned from his foreign tour was concerned with home affairs. His sister and Queen tried to poison him at the banquet which celebrated his safe arrival. As on other occasions, the poison did him no harm; either because of the daily dose of antidote or because he was naturally immune.

That evening Queen Laodice was put to death, and with her many of her courtiers.

The widower did not marry again. If even his sister would betray him, then no woman was worthy of his trust. There was no point in repeating the unsuccessful experiment with his younger sisters; they remained, unmarried, in the hill-top castle to which they had been confined since they reached adolescence. Henceforth there was no Queen of Pontus. Mithradates was not thereby condemned to celibacy; but from now on his companions were either oriental odalisques, bred to seclusion, or Greek courtesans.

It is said that during the year 99 Mithradates encountered the most famous Roman of the day. Certainly Caius Marius was visiting Asia at that time, but he was not engaged on a diplomatic mission. At Rome his party had lost the elections, and from sheer pique he went into self-imposed exile, ostensibly to consult the famous oracles of the East. Marius is alleged to have divined the greatness of the foreign King, and to have warned him sternly: 'You must obey the Romans, unless you can make yourself stronger than they.'

This does not sound convincing. Mithradates, now aged 33, had ruled in Pontus for the last twelve years without displaying any remarkable qualities or any particular enmity to Rome; there was no reason why a Roman should warn him. If a meeting did in fact take place perhaps Romans of the Popular faction might afterwards invent the story to show that the old Popular leader was as farseeing as his famous rival Sulla.

As a matter of fact, just about this time Mithradates made his first cautious move against Rome, where acute party-strife was leading up to the great conflict known as the Social War. The tribune Saturninus had raised an armed revolt actually within the City; the revolt was quelled only at the cost of heavy casualties, themselves the beginning of blood-feuds which endured for many generations. When news of these troubles reached Mithradates they emboldened him to approach King Nicomedes of Bithynia with a project for their joint aggrandisement.

While every Roman soldier was busy picking his side for the coming civil war the combined armies of Bithynia and Pontus overran Paphlagonia and Galatia for the second time, and in addition Cappadocia. This deed was an open breach of their treaties with Rome, which forbade them to enlarge their frontiers without previous consent from the Senate. But they knew that no Senator would have leisure to inquire into their doings for so long as the political crisis lasted, and they trusted to bribing themselves out of trouble when in the end a Senatorial commission should find time to visit Asia.

The King of Pontus

Paphlagonia and Galatia collapsed at once; but in Cappadocia Mithradates had to deal with his sister, the elder Laodice, still Queen-regent for her son Ariarathes. She had her share of the family competence; her army resisted until a truce was arranged between her brother and his nephew.

After negotiations it was agreed that the two Kings should meet for a private interview, in an open plain where their supporters could watch from a distance to see fair play. Before the meeting both were searched for concealed weapons. But Mithradates had strapped a sharp little knife to his penis, where it was hidden by his baggy Persian trousers. He cut the throat of his nephew, the unlucky young King of Cappadocia.

Even after this setback Laodice was determined to remain a Queen. With great presence of mind she offered her hand and realm to the rival invader, the widowed King Nicomedes. Bithynia and Cappadocia were united, and though Laodice had lost her regency she was now Queen-consort of both. Baffled, Mithradates withdrew.

For the next four years the allied Kings ruled supreme in Asia; then the ruling faction in Rome had leisure to take note of what had happened in the east. A Roman propraetor was sent to recall all client-Kings to their treaty obligations. The Roman envoy brought no troops with him, and his rank in the official hierarchy of the republic was not of the highest. But he was the most famous general of the younger generation; his mere coming was a reminder of threatened war.

In 95 L. Cornelius Sulla was already known as the daring soldier who had captured King Jugurtha of Numidia, and the daring lieutenant of Marius at the great defeats of the German invaders. He carried matters with a high hand. He did not argue, and he would not accept bribes. Briefly he commanded the Kings to withdraw from all their conquests, not bothering to mention what would happen to them if they remained defiant.

Panic-stricken, King Nicomedes immediately promised to do all that was commanded. Without his support Mithradates was too weak to challenge Rome; he also must yield. On the retreat of the invading armies Galatia and Paphlagonia returned to congenial anarchy; but in Cappadocia Sulla took steps to set up a new administration. Since the royal house was extinct the

43

native nobility were commanded to elect a new King from
among themselves. One Ariobarzanes was chosen, whose name
indicates his Persian descent. He was never popular among his
subjects, and kept his throne only with Roman support.

Mithradates considered that he had been betrayed by the
pusillanimous Nicomedes. He broke with his worthless ally, and
for ever after was the foe of Bithynia. Another power was eager
for his alliance. He married his 13-year-old daughter Cleopatra
to the 40-year-old King Tigranes of Armenia. Tigranes was an
ambitious and warlike prince, who was extending his dominions southward at the expense of the decaying Kingdom of Syria.

The first result of this dynastic marriage was that in 93 the
Armenians invaded Cappadocia. The miserable Ariobarzanes
fled all the way to Rome. It was evident that the Armenians
were acting for Mithradates, since the regent they installed was
his old friend Gordius. Yet when Rome reacted neither Armenia
nor Pontus would face war. Sulla, still in the east, raised a force
of local levies, stiffened by the single legion from Cilicia. Before
his advance the Armenians retired, until Cappadocia was once
more governed in the name of the fugitive Ariobarzanes.

In 91 an incursion of northern barbarians occupied the
Roman garrison of Macedonia (it was rumoured that these barbarians had been hired by Mithradates); and a revolt of the
Italian communities, the famous Social War, kept the main
Roman army busy at home. At this juncture died King Nicomedes II, leaving as heir to Bithynia an incompetent and
vicious tyrant. Although Nicomedes III was the only legitimate
son of the late King his subjects were reluctant to obey him,
and his bastard half-brother Socrates had a considerable
following in the country.

Socrates fled eastward to Pontus, and returned with a Pontic
army. While he overran the open country the legitimate King
shut himself up behind the strong walls of Nicomedia. At the
same time the Armenians once more invaded Cappadocia.

This time the Armenians set up as their puppet-King a
young man known as Ariarathes, who claimed to be a sixth,
previously unknown, brother of the five sons murdered years
ago by their mother Queen Nysa. It was common gossip that he
was really Arcathius, son of King Mithradates and his sister-
Queen Laodice.

The King of Pontus

Two years later the irrepressible Romans were as strong as they had ever been, and it was once more time for little barbarian kinglets to obey. Half the Italian rebels had changed sides when offered Roman citizenship; the other half had suffered a series of bloody defeats. A Roman Senator was sent out to inquire into the condition of Asia, and to restore stolen Kingdoms to their rightful possessors.

In their choice of an envoy the Senate displayed little tact, and even less wisdom. Manius Aquilius was the son of the Roman commissioner who had first organized the province of Asia. The father had been notorious for dishonest avarice; he took bribes from every Asiatic ruler, and even when bribed was too crooked to give value for money. Mithradates Euergetes had paid heavily for Phrygia, and been cheated of it because the Senate refused to ratify the bargain. But the bribe had never been returned, and in Pontus they felt a grievance.

All that Aquilius the younger knew about the East was that his father had made a fortune there. He sat waiting in Pergamum for the bribes to come in, and was dismayed when they did not.

This generation of allied Kings knew more about the Roman constitution than their fathers. There was nothing to be gained by bribing a commissioner whose arrangements might be overruled by the Senate; and no one was rich enough to bribe a majority in a house of 600 Senators. The only way to deal with the Romans, as perhaps Marius had said to Mithradates, was to obey their commands or to defeat them.

Tigranes of Armenia shrank from all-out war with Rome. Ravaged Cappadocia was not really important to him; he had only conquered it to please his father-in-law. As soon as he received the Roman ultimatum he ordered his troops to retire, and Ariobarzanes was restored to his rickety throne. Unsupported by Armenia, Mithradates must also give way. He was not officially committed to war with Bithynia, for the Pontic troops who followed Socrates were in name volunteers. But his prestige among his own subjects was very dear to him, and it would be damaged if he openly obeyed the commands of a Roman envoy. He saw a way to wind up the dangerous campaign without loss of face, and took it ruthlessly. Socrates died suddenly. With the pretender out of the way the civil war in

45

Bithynia came to an end, and the Pontic 'volunteers' went home.

The allied Kings had obeyed the commands of Rome as soon as they had been issued. But Aquilius was not a penny the richer than when he had landed in Asia. Furthermore, to meet the stress of invasion Nicomedes and Ariobarzanes had borrowed heavily from Roman financiers, and had promised rich bribes to many Senators on condition they were restored to their Kingdoms by Roman arms. Now they explained that their lands had been ravaged, and that their backers must wait for repayment. Aquilius would not wait. Since no one would bribe him he turned to the alternative which would suggest itself to any Roman, the plunder of successful war. Pontus had not been ravaged for more than a generation, and Nicomedes could if he wished find an excuse for war in the support afforded by Mithradates to the pretender. Let Nicomedes send his fleet to plunder the wealthy cities of the Pontic coast; while the single legion commanded by Cassius, Roman proconsul in Asia, moved up to Bithynia to protect him from reprisals.

Nicomedes was reluctant to set out on this adventure. But unless he obeyed orders his Roman creditors threatened to foreclose on his Kingdom, and perhaps news reached him that the Pontic fleet was absent in the Chersonese. Early in 88 he did as he had been told. His mercenary foot marched eastward over the frontier, while his fleet, unopposed, plundered the undefended Pontic harbours as far as Amastris.

Mithradates complied with the treaty which forbade him to make war on another ally of Rome. He did not resist the advance of forces whose movements were directed by a Roman envoy; he merely sent an ambassador to protest personally to Aquilius. The ambassador, the usual Greek expert on foreign affairs, begged Aquilius to order Nicomedes to withdraw.

The Bithynian navy withdrew, but with an immense hoard of plunder. Mithradates asked for restitution of the stolen property; and as a hint that he was not entirely powerless once more loosed on Cappadocia his son, the false Ariarathes. Aquilius replied that the Bithynians had carried out a legitimate reprisal on Pontus, which was guilty of supporting Socrates. The Pontic ambassador was expelled from the Roman camp, and the invaders prepared openly for another raid. Mithradates saw that unless he met force with force he would be robbed of all he possessed.

The Roman Senate did not regard the King of Pontus as an enemy. He had done no harm to Rome, and no serious harm to the Roman-protected Kingdoms. Twice he had withdrawn his troops from conquered lands at the mere request of Roman envoys, without waiting for a threat of force. Aquilius had not been commissioned to make war on him; all the bloodshed which followed was caused only by his private greed.

Aquilius may be pardoned for underestimating the power of the victim he intended to plunder. Mithradates was now 43 years of age, and for more than twenty years he had ruled in Pontus as the client of Rome. It was common knowledge that he hankered after complete independence; but when Rome was at her weakest, during the crisis of the Social War, he had not dared to move. Now the Romans were winning back the mastery of Italy, and soon their main army would be free for adventure overseas. Mithradates would send another protest, perhaps he would send ambassadors directly to the Senate; but his past conduct showed that he would never face a legion in the open field.

Nevertheless, in the summer of 88 the long-suffering client-King turned to bay. As the forces of Pontus mobilized the Roman commanders in Asia saw with delight a prospect of easy plunder. To make quite sure of crushing the little Kingdom they mustered four separate armies at different points on the frontier. Aquilius, at the head of 40,000 mercenaries and local allies, supported the 60,000 Bithynians whom Nicomedes led eastward along the coast. Cassius, proconsul in Asia, led another 40,000 men; he proposed to invade from the south-west, from the frontier of Bithynia and Galatia, and the nucleus of his powerful army was the Roman legion which was the standing garrison of Asia. The propraetor in Cilicia, Oppius, with his legion and additional levies, another 40,000 men in all, planned to reach the heart of inland Pontus by crossing the mountain frontier of Cappadocia. In all, 180,000 men were on the march, though only 12,000 of them were true Roman soldiers. In addition, a squadron of Greek warships in Roman service cruised at the entrance to the Bosphorus, as backing for the Bithynian navy.

It should have been a walk-over.

II

The Liberator of Hellas

Before relating the events of this war it would be well to
describe the character of the forces involved. Ancient
historians give very high figures for the numbers of men
in the field; and it is important to remember that some formations were of much greater military value than others. It is
possible that Appian in particular exaggerated the number of
men engaged; but unless we follow his estimate we have no
estimate at all. It is on the whole more likely that he gives
'ration-strengths', which would include muleteers, porters, and
servants, than that he tells downright lies; and that when he
totted up his totals he was generous in arriving at a round
number. After all, every historian likes to remind his readers
that the story he is relating is the story of a great war.

If in fact Appian exaggerated, he probably did so consistently.
He may well be right about the relative strength of the armies,
though the actual figures for each may be too large.

When Alexander the Great conquered the east he employed
the standard Greek tactics of his day; and after 250 years those
tactics still held the field. The Greek warrior was essentially a
spearman, protected by a large stout shield. In addition he
carried a sword, and wore helmet, corselet, and greaves. But
this auxiliary equipment was not important. Herodotus,
describing the gallant stand of the Spartans at Thermopylae,
says that after their spears were broken they fought on with
swords, fists, and teeth, as though these were equally effective.
The short Greek sword was the easily concealed weapon of the
assassin, of little worth on the battlefield. But the shield was as
important as the spear. A tyrant could disarm a whole city by
tricking the citizens into giving up their shields, though they
still retained spears, swords, and armour. A shieldless man could

48

not stand in the line of battle. That was why a fugitive who threw away his shield to run faster had disgraced himself; he had thrown away his own value as a soldier.

In the first century B.C. some Greeks still fought as their ancestors had fought at Marathon, 400 years before. Drawn up shoulder to shoulder in a line of six ranks these 'hoplites' (fully-armed men) wielded a six-foot spear in the right hand while the left managed the shield, now sheathed in metal and so very heavy. But these were no longer the characteristic infantry of the Hellenistic world, and to distinguish them from the rival formation they were known as 'Chalcaspides', brazen shields.

The Thebans and Macedonians had carried the tactics of heavy spear-armed infantry to its logical conclusion, to produce the phalanx. In this ponderous formation the men were packed very close together in sixteen ranks. They carried pikes twenty-two feet long, which of course needed both hands to hold them. In consequence the pikeman bore his small leather shield attached to the upper part of his left arm; in this position it protected, not its bearer, but the man on his left.

The phalanx was the striking-force of every Hellenistic army; though its deep formation covered a very small front, so that to protect its flanks the line was usually prolonged with chalcaspides. It was handled as a single tactical formation of up to 16,000 men. Its charge, when properly delivered, was irresistible. Before a thick column of close-packed shields, with eight rows of pikeheads projecting before the front rank, even Roman legions must yield ground.

But the clumsy formation had many disadvantages. The close order demanded very well-drilled men; an untrained phalanx soon dissolved into a mob. Since every man must move at the same speed as his fellows the slightest obstacle broke the array. The pikes projected only in front, so the phalanx was vulnerable to attack from the flank; especially from the right flank, where the right-hand file were not protected by shields. Above all, every phalangite must be a brave man of steady nerves; for though his offensive power was very great he could do nothing to defend himself. He could not parry with the shield strapped immovably to his left arm; there was no room for him to dodge; his long pike projected between the heads of the men before him, and could not be moved to meet attack

D   49

from any quarter except the immediate front. If he saw a javelin coming he could only set his teeth and wait for it.

If in the heat of action a phalanx broke, there must follow a ghastly massacre. A pike twenty-two feet long was no help to an individual unprotected by his neighbours; an adversary had only to dodge past the distant spearpoint and he had everything in his favour. Phalangites were supposed to carry swords, though many found them an encumbrance on the march and got rid of them; the little shield strapped to the upper arm was no protection at close quarters.

Besides these two forms of heavy infantry a standard Greek army would contain light troops. Peltasts were equipped with light shields and light armour. Their function was to occupy broken ground; their offensive weapons, besides the inconsiderable sword, might be either a hoplite spear or a sheaf of javelins. True Greeks used the bow only in hunting; but many of the barbarians of Asia were archers. They, and other barbarians who used the sling, would be found as mercenaries guarding the outposts or scouting ahead of the main body.

In the ancient world, where the stirrup was still unknown, cavalry were never supreme on the battlefield. A cavalier without stirrups may be pushed over the tail of his horse if he meets an adversary full tilt. All the same, though they did not win pitched battles, cavalry were important; a horseman armed with javelins or arrows could damage the phalanx without risk to himself, and if the hostile foot wavered he might charge home with the sword. The generals of those days seldom depended on a line of communications; food was usually collected by foraging in the district where the army lay encamped. If the horse of one army was unquestionably superior, its adversary could not send out small detachments to forage.

The Greeks were not a horsey people. Alexander led Macedonian squadrons, but after his day the cavalry of a Greek army was usually composed of barbarian mercenaries.

So far we have been discussing the armed forces of Hellenistic states; soldiers of this kind made up the bulk of the armies engaged in Asia in the year 88. The contingents furnished by Bithynia, Cappadocia, and Galatia consisted of mercenaries, Greek or barbarian, of the same type as the mercenaries hired by the King of Pontus. But these contingents would never have

The Liberator of Hellas

dared to undertake their invasion if they had not been supported by a small number of Roman troops. It is time to describe the quite different tactics and organization of the Roman army.

This was an astonishingly specialized force, made up entirely of infantry of the line. In practice Rome no longer enforced universal military service, though every citizen was still liable to serve if called upon; but the army contained only genuine Roman citizens, every man a volunteer who had signed on for a long-term engagement. It was the custom for young men of good family, who intended to take up a political career, to serve a few campaigns as horsemen. But these 'knights' were no longer organized into squadrons; they were employed individually as gallopers or staff officers. Except for these few knights every Roman who adopted the profession of arms must serve in a legion, and in reckoning the strength of an army only legions were counted. Of course the commander of these legions would have at his disposal cavalry, light infantry, engineers, and a baggage train; but these men would be either mercenaries hired from abroad or the contingents of client states bound by treaty to furnish them.

A legion was quite a different kind of fighting-machine from a body of Greek hoplites, whether a phalanx or a line of chalcaspides. The essential difference was that the spear was not used in the Roman army; every legionary was a trained swordsman, and his drill had taught him to defend himself as an individual, without relying on the shields of his neighbours. The pointed, double-edged broadsword which he carried was a much more efficient weapon than the clumsy knife of the Greeks. On his left arm he bore a large square shield which protected him from neck to knee; but this shield, of leather, was light enough to be moved to parry a blow. The spearless Roman could move it, since his left hand was free. He went into battle carrying inside his shield two javelins; but he was not expected to skirmish with these heavy missiles, made more of iron than of wood. They were thrown in quick succession, at very short range, just before he closed with the hostile line.

The legion was divided into ten cohorts, each of three maniples, each of two centuries. On paper this adds up to 6,000 men; but the legion was raised as a single formation, and no

51

depot kept up a constant stream of reinforcements. In practice
the century was usually reckoned at eighty men, and a long
campaign would further reduce its numbers.

The tactical unit was the maniple drawn up in three ranks. A
Roman commander liked to have three lines of maniples, one
behind the other. But if he needed to extend his line the
maniples might be arrayed in a chequer-board formation, the
second line blocking the gaps in the first. There was always a
considerable interval between one maniple and the next in line.

The Roman legionary, unlike the Greek spearman, did not
stand shoulder to shoulder with his comrades, protected on his
shieldless right by the shield of his right-hand neighbour. He
stood at a full arm's-length from his fellows, and with his own
sword and shield was expected to defend himself from attack
from any quarter as though he were alone on the battlefield.

In this light flexible formation Roman foot could take
ground much more speedily than close-packed Greeks, who
could not run without stumbling over the ranks in front of
them. There was the further advantage that a Roman legion of
about 4,800 men in chequer-board formation would have about
550 men in the front rank, holding, with the intervals between
maniples, about 1,800 yards of front; while a Greek phalanx of
16,000 men would have 1,000 in the front rank, but they would
occupy only about 700 yards.

At an epoch when serious fighting meant hand-to-hand
fighting a man who must use one hand to hoist himself over an
obstacle was at a tremendous disadvantage. Therefore any
physical obstacle, which must be climbed by the attackers, was
of great value to the defence. Every civilized army was accustomed to fortify its camp with at least a simple bank and ditch.
The Romans, expert in trench warfare, added to the bank a
stout palisade; each legionary carried two stakes on the march,
and whenever he camped, even for one night, his first task was
to dig the earthwork and plant his stakes on the crest. A Roman
commander took it for granted that his camp would be safe so
long as his men were willing to hold the palisade; only if the
troops were so demoralized that they flinched from their entrenchments could a Roman camp fall to enemy assault. Greek
camps were not quite so strong, but if they were bravely defended even Romans would think twice before assaulting one.

The Liberator of Hellas

It followed from this superiority of the defensive that a pitched battle could be fought only if both armies were willing to fight it. A general might draw out his men in line of battle, but if the other side remained behind their bank and ditch he dared not attack. In that case he might shout insults to his foes, in the hope that they would lose their tempers. The point may be illustrated by a famous anecdote of the Social War. Marius, leading a weak Roman army, sat tight in his camp. The Italian commander, an old comrade in arms, shouted to him: 'Marius, if you are such a great general, why don't you come out and fight me?' To which Marius replied: 'If you are such a great general, you just make me fight against my will.' No battle took place.

Stone walls, of course, were even more invulnerable than a palisade. The siege of a walled city was always a difficult and dangerous operation. In theory engines could in the end batter down the strongest wall; but in practice that took a very long time. Of course if even a few of the attackers got on the ramparts the advantage of the defence vanished at once; the whole circuit must be held, complete. When a city was taken by assault it was nearly always because a few attackers had climbed up an unguarded stretch of wall. The defence must always have a great many sentinels on watch; if the garrison were short-handed that could be very exhausting.

In spite of all the ingenuity and effort of Greek engineers, few cities were captured by any other method than starvation.

In naval affairs there was no distinction between Greek and Roman. Both used ships of the same pattern, manned by sailors of Greek birth or by Syrians who followed the technical methods of Greece. One fact must be continually borne in mind, especially by English readers brought up on the doctrine that the stronger fleet can win absolute command of the sea. Ancient warships resembled much more a modern fighter aircraft than a three-decker of Nelson's day. They were designed to go out to fight, and then come back to shelter. The most convincing explanation of the difference between a quinquereme and a trireme is that it refers to the number of rowers at each oar, not to banks of oars one above the other. If the oars were superimposed in banks they must have been of different length, and could not have been rowed in time together. But whether a quinquereme was moved by five banks of oars or by five men to each oar, it was crowded with rowers.

Furthermore, oars cannot be rowed together unless all the rowlocks are in a straight line from bow to stern; but the sides of a sea-going ship are curved. In the galleys of the sixteenth century, of which accurate models and plans have come down to us, a rectangular framework was fixed above the hull, to provide a straight setting for the rowlocks. If this device was used also in the galleys of antiquity the result would be a very unseaworthy and unstable vessel.

In fact the classical galley was extremely unseaworthy. Every war-fleet which encountered bad weather suffered heavily from shipwreck. But the most important fact limiting the efficiency of a first-century squadron was that the overcrowded triremes could carry only water enough for a few days at sea; and that the crew could not cook a hot meal, or even stretch out at full-length to sleep, until their ship was drawn up on the strand or anchored in harbour.

Thus at this period even the strongest navy could not achieve complete command of the sea. After voyaging for four or five days of increasing hardship the crews must go ashore for a rest. A particular harbour might be blockaded, by ships based on a strand only a few miles away; a narrow channel might be held by ships lying permanently at anchor in it. But open water could not be denied even to a much weaker foe, who could dodge his way through by short voyages while the stronger fleet was resting.

In the spring of 88, four armies of the type described above were poised for the invasion of Pontus. To the Romans the expedition was a plundering raid, in which they did not expect to meet troublesome resistance. They did not bother to combine their forces; but sent on in advance King Nicomedes and his Bithynians, because they were already mobilized.

Mithradates was waiting for them, determined to make a fight of it. He had spent his treasure lavishly in hiring mercenaries, and his native subjects had rallied to the heir of their ancient dynasty; his army numbered 250,000 foot, including light-armed skirmishers and the drivers of the baggage-train. These were mostly Greek mercenaries of the ordinary type, as good as the Bithynian mercenaries but no better. But his horse, to the number of 40,000, were either stout Cappadocians of Persian descent, fighting for their hereditary lord, or fierce Scythian mercenaries from the steppe. Both Scythians and Cappadocians outclassed the casual mercenary troopers enlisted by the Romans.

Since the phalanx reigned supreme on every Hellenistic battlefield intelligent Hellenistic statesmen were always trying to find some way to beat it. About this time Parthians and Armenians were experimenting with *cataphractarii*, very heavy cavalry; in fact they were so heavily armoured and encumbered with such long lances (*contoi*, barge-poles, these were nicknamed by slangy Greeks) that only exceptionally big horses could carry them. Heavy cavalry armed with long lances might break up a phalanx; but only if they themselves were formed in such close order that they became practically another phalanx on horseback, as unwieldly and difficult to drill as their adversaries on foot. In any case, the very big weight-carrying horses were found only in Parthia. Since Mithradates had none of them he could not use cataphractarii.

The immediate successors of Alexander had used elephants with some success. But by the first century these were obsolete. The beasts were too intelligent to obey orders blindly, and refused to commit suicide by charging into the pikes if the phalanx stood firm. They were still occasionally used in war, to batter in the gate of a besieged city or as a screen against cavalry; for horses who see elephants for the first time usually bolt in panic. Some writers say Mithradates had a few of them, which he must have fetched all the way from India. But the fact is doubtful, and if he possessed them he did not employ them in pitched battles.

All the same, Mithradates had his secret weapon; or rather, he had revived a very ancient form of armament. His army contained a corps of 130 chariots, their wheels armed with projecting scythe-blades. These chariots were not designed to carry heavy-armed warriors; they themselves were used as missiles. Taking a long run over level ground, the driver flogged his team of four horses into a frenzied gallop which no obstacle could stop; he then steered them into the serried pike-heads. If the phalanx stood firm four dead horses and the wreckage of the chariot made a gap in the row of spears into which infantry might follow; but it was hoped that the enemy would flinch from the collision, breaking formation without destroying the chariot.

Mithradates had been brought up to think that a great King was too great to fight in person. Nevertheless, it is really remarkable, and a proof of exceptional self-control, that he, the famous horseman, the best shot with arrow or javelin in all Asia, did not aspire to lead his army in the field. He had no military experience, but he knew himself to be a good judge of men; he picked sound professional generals, and allowed them to conduct the campaign. Two brothers, Greeks, Neoptolemus and Archelaus, were his chief commanders. The chariot-corps was commanded by another Greek mercenary, Craterus. Dorylaus, son of his father's general, led the phalanx. Ten thousand Armenian horse, the pick of the cavalry, were commanded by Arcathius, the young prince who had attempted to rule Cappadocia under the name of Ariarathes. This last appointment is further evidence of the unprejudiced outlook of Mithradates. His sons were normally the most dangerous enemies of a Hellenistic King; few monarchs who did not themselves intend to take the field would have dared to entrust a large body of troops to a prince of the blood. Here again Mithradates guessed right. Arcathius never intrigued against his father; or perhaps it is only that he died young, before he had time to plot treason.

The enormous army of Pontus, far bigger than anything the Romans had expected, mustered slowly at Sinope. With invasion menacing three widely distant points of the frontier the main body must be held back to await developments; but they must at once deal with King Nicomedes of Bithynia, who was ravaging the western sea-board. While the slow-moving phalanx remained to defend Sinope, the light infantry, the chariots, and the best of the cavalry set out to oppose the Bithynians.

Near the river Amnias, in Paphlagonia, the two armies collided. The encounter brought on a straggling, unpremeditated battle, in which the Pontic troops fought well and enjoyed more than their fair share of luck. When Nicomedes attacked a Pontic outpost Neoptolemus reinforced the defenders; presently all the foot on both sides were engaged. Pontic light infantry scattered the Bithynian skirmishers, but could make no impression on the phalanx. Seeing his foot give way, Arcathius charged; though for cavalry to charge an unbroken phalanx was to invite heavy casualties with no hope of victory. But as the day wore on the nimble light infantry completely surrounded the Bithynians, whose phalanx was compelled to form front in every direction. In this posture they made a perfect target for the chariots, whose drivers charged home. Now luck favoured Pontus. Never again did these chariots produce any military effect; but in this first battle, where victory was so urgently needed, the Bithynian phalanx broke under their impact.

A broken phalanx always lost heavily; the Bithynians were already surrounded, and their cavalry had been driven from the field. King Nicomedes with his bodyguard cut a way out of the trap; but without horse or light infantry he could not disengage his foot, he could not even man the palisade of his fortified camp. While he galloped westward his hoplites fought on until more than half of them were slain; the rest surrendered. By evening the Pontic army had taken thousands of prisoners, the complete camp and baggage-train of the Bithynians, and, best of all, their rich war-chest.

The demoralization of the Bithynian mercenaries was strikingly displayed a few days later, when 800 of their horse bumped into 100 Pontic cavalry (tough Sarmatians from the steppe) and fled disgracefully, leaving many prisoners.

This overthrow of a numerically superior enemy brought Mithradates great prestige. Although not a single Roman soldier had been engaged it was seen by all Asia as a Roman defeat. The three Roman generals, as dismayed as their allies, at once began to retire.

When the survivors of the Bithynian phalanx were brought before Mithradates he set them free, and gave them money for their journey home. He had gone to war with the slogan of death to all Romans but peace to every Asiatic. Naturally this generous action won him many friends, but it is not likely that his prisoners retired thus early from the war. They were professional mercenaries, not patriotic Bithynians. Most of them enlisted in the Pontic army.

King Nicomedes fled to Manius Aquilius, the nearest Roman commander. But when Neoptolemus approached he resumed his flight until he reached a Roman army farther to the rear, that of Cassius. Evidently he was a shrewd judge of military form; for when Neoptolemus caught up with the retreating Aquilius he won an overwhelming victory. Aquilius lost 10,000 men killed, a quarter of his force; the rest scattered in rout, and even the Roman camp was captured. Almost alone Aquilius fled over the river Sangarius to Pergamum.

At news of this second defeat the troops of Oppius deserted their standards without striking a blow. Oppius and his Roman staff tried to gather another army in Phrygia, but soon gave up the attempt and sought refuge in Apamaea. King Nicomedes shut himself up in the strong fortress of Pergamum; but Aquilius had already decided that the capital of the Roman province could not be defended, for the citizens would betray their hated masters. Aquilius fled shamefully to the coast, and Nicomedes followed.

The flight of Oppius ended at Laodicea-on-Lycus. He had with him a small force of mercenaries, and was prepared to defend the town. Then Mithradates appeared in person before the walls, to proclaim that the citizens would suffer no harm if they handed over the Roman fugitives. The Laodiceans accordingly persuaded the mercenaries to desert, and themselves delivered Oppius to the King; to add insult to injury they compelled his lictors to march before him, so that he entered captivity in the full state of a Roman magistrate.

Aquilius nearly got away. He reached Mytilene, where only the sea separated him from Italy. There the citizens seized him and handed him over to his pursuers.

When, about this time, Pergamum opened its gates, Mithradates might call himself King of all Asia. Two victories, won by his generals while he sat quietly in Sinope, had destroyed the power of Rome in every land east of the Aegean. Among his captives were two Roman magistrates, and he got the utmost publicity out of these rare trophies by displaying them all over the conquered provinces. Oppius marched through city squares until the whole world knew he was a prisoner; but he was an honest man, who had not especially oppressed his subjects, and after a time the King freed him from his chains and kept him at court as something between a hostage and a curio. Aquilius met a harsher fate. He was displayed throughout Asia, bound to the back of a donkey; when the interest of the crowd was sated he was brought to Pergamum, until recently his capital, and there publicly put to death. As a token that he was being punished for extortion molten gold was poured down his throat until he died.

It was not a very important addition to these victories that the Roman fleet stationed in the Bosphorus mutinied, and came over *en bloc* to Pontus. Now the Pontic fleet, about 400 vessels large and small, commanded the Euxine, the Bosphorus, the Propontis and the Hellespont, and might be used for siege-operations in the Aegean.

While his generals reduced the few remaining centres of resistance Mithradates made a state progress through the conquered territories. He knew that he had not really gained these cities by victory in war; the citizens had changed sides because they hated the Romans. If he wanted to keep the great dominion which had come to him as the reward of two weeks' fighting he must devise a policy that would content them. During the summer of 88 the Persian from Pontus, in trousers and tiara, built up his reputation as the champion of Greek culture against the alien power of Rome.

He toured the Ionian cities, Magnesia, Ephesus, Mytilene. Everywhere he was welcomed as a liberator, and he threw himself into the role. He abolished the oligarchic constitutions set up under Roman influence, and gave power to the democracy. In the political vocabulary of that time this did not mean that he gave votes to everyone, or even to all males. It means that he specifically gave to the poor power over the rich; the nearest modern equivalent is not liberty but the dictatorship of the proletariat. With the closing of the Aegean to merchant shipping the international slave-trade had vanished, but Mithradates went out of his way to encourage the freeing of peasant-serfs. By his orders the cities enfranchized their resident aliens, a numerous class; for it was rare to acquire the citizenship of a Greek town save by inheritance, and a family of immigrant traders might do business for generations without being granted civic rights.

In spite of these measures the rich were not bitterly opposed to him; for he had taken so much war-booty that he could cancel all debts owed to the late Roman government and remit the customary tribute for the next five years. By the time he returned to Pergamum, where he had decided to set up his capital, he was immensely popular.

In Pergamum he ruled in great splendour, after the Greek fashion. Official ceremonies were graced by a Greek consort, though she was not exactly a Queen. The city of Stratonicea had remained faithful to the Roman alliance until Mithradates himself approached with his main army. At the surrender he rode in leading his troops. In the crowd which watched his entry he noticed a pretty face; but even after Monime the daughter of Philopoemen had been offered the very large sum of 15,000 gold pieces she still refused to be his mistress. The girl stood out for marriage-lines; and though she did not get them the eventual compromise was very much in her favour. She was granted the right to wear the diadem, and all the public honours of a Queen-consort; but her rank was local and acting, effective only in Greek cities. In native Pontus they took no notice of her, and her name was not mentioned, as that of a true Queen would have been, in public decrees.

Her undistinguished father was made governor of Ephesus, a much bigger city than his native place. In Pergamum Monime reigned as Queen; while her barbarian lover attended performances in the Greek theatre, and even drove a team of sixteen horses abreast in competition with noble Greeks, during the chariot-races of the Greek hippodrome.

In January 88 Mithradates had been a petty client-King on the fronge of civilization; by midsummer he was ruler of all Asia, from Taurus to the Propontis, with Roman magistrates led captive before him. All his greatness was based on two lucky victories, won by mercenary generals in his absence. But the Greeks had found a champion to deliver them from the tyranny of Rome, and the snowball of his power continued to grow.

But the republic of Rhodes, on his south-eastern border, had a tradition of enmity to Kings. With great courage the little state remained faithful to the Roman alliance. Mithradates began to gather his fleet in order to besiege it, meanwhile looking round for some method of binding his present flighty allies firmly to his cause. For the moment Rome was occupied by a civil war between the Popular party led by old Marius and the Senatorial oligarchy led by Sulla; but soon whichever side was victorious would send out an army to reconquer the lost

dominions. The Ionian cities must be bound to the novel cause
of Greek freedom by some deed of blood from which there
could be no drawing back. In secrecy Mithradates prepared his
next move.

The move he decided on was a rash doubling of the stakes, in
which he threw away the offer of a valuable alliance. Many
Italian communities were still in arms against the domination
of Rome; others, beaten in the field, would rise again on the
promise of help from abroad. But while an embassy from the
Italian rebels was actually on its way to Pergamum Mithradates plotted the simultaneous massacre of every Italian in
Asia. Perhaps, once he had decided to kill all Romans, he had
no choice in the matter. Even in Italy Roman citizenship went
very much by chance; there were Roman citizens in every
Italian community, and crowds of non-citizens in Rome herself. The public executioner could hardly examine his victims'
papers before he cut their throats. Any Italian could be recognized by his barbarous speech.

Therefore the order went out all over Asia, in the utmost
secrecy. On a given day the local authorities in every town
must arrange the killing of every stranger who spoke Italian.
Since the only possible test was speech no attention was to be
paid to status; even slaves, if Italian was their tongue, must be
killed. But only Italians were to suffer; their servants, if they
did not speak Italian, should be spared.

Racial hatred did not come naturally to Greeks. Many Greek
cities had a bloody record of merciless civil war, and most of
them cherished an hereditary animosity against some Greek
neighbour and rival. But to murder a man because he spoke the
wrong language was not a Greek thing. Barbarians should be
pitied and despised; to hate them was to give them altogether
too much importance.

Also, the new governments of the Ionian cities were composed
of intelligent men, who understood the consequences of such an
atrocity. By favour of Mithradates they had overthrown the
oligarchical adherents of Rome; a day might come when it
would be expedient to change sides again.

Nevertheless, when it came to the point Mithradates was
obeyed by every city in Asia. Only the men of Tralles tried to
avoid personal bloodguilt while following the instructions of

their new ruler; they called in a Paphlagonian bandit to do their killing for them. This Theophilus massacred the Italians of Tralles in circumstances of peculiar savagery. When he cut off the hands of his victims as they clung to the image within the Temple of Concord the citizens looked on without offering to interfere. Elsewhere the massacre was conducted with gusto, evidence of the hatred a single generation of Roman rule had instilled into the minds of her new subjects. At Ephesus and Pergamum fugitives were murdered within the most sacred shrines; at Caunium, a city recently delivered by the Romans from subjection to Rhodes, the programme of execution was carefully devised by an expert in mental cruelty. After the Italians had been assembled the children were killed before the eyes of their parents, then the women, and lastly the men. Everywhere burial was denied to the victims, which to a Greek or Roman mind was a greater outrage than death by torture.

All Italian property was of course confiscated to the royal treasury, and all slaves owned by Italians received their freedom. From this unexpected source Mithradates received a reinforcement of most faithful soldiers; no less than 6,000 able-bodied freedmen were recruited into his phalanx. It is said that in the massacre there perished 80,000 Italian men, women, and children; even if this figure is exaggerated the owners of 6,000 young men must have made up a large community.

Mithradates had completed his programme. He was supreme from Syria to Europe. He did not assume the title of Great King, King of Kings; such a claim might have antagonized his valued ally the King of Armenia. But to his Greek subjects he was Xerxes or Darius come again; though he might call the governors whom he set over his new provinces by the non-committal name of Eparch, the rest of the world referred to them as satraps.

From his great palace at Pergamum he controlled every department of state, himself working hard at the business of government. Every evening there was a state banquet, at which the entertainment was varied to suit all tastes. Usually these suppers were enlivened by the conversation of literary men, but sometimes they became crude drinking-bouts; once the King personally competed in an eating-contest, and won it; overcoming even professional boxers in training, proverbially the

great gluttons of the Greek world. The usual palace parties
followed in every particular the Greek code of manners; save
that the King himself reclined in Persian trousers, his sword at
his waist and his bow and quiver at hand. The beautiful
Monime reclined beside him, in everything except lawful marriage Queen of Asia. The new régime was popular, efficient,
secure.

Although in most things Mithradates was his own minister,
in one field of government he took no part. The public
opinion of Asia did not expect a great ruler to lead his own
armies. A King should choose able generals, and himself keep
away from the fighting. It seems odd to us of the present day
that a King who was first of all a great conqueror should never
have seen battle; his own subjects thought it more honourable
that the monarch should sit in his capital while lesser men
extended his dominions.

During the late summer of 88 it seemed that the dominions of
Mithradates were expanding without effort from himself or
from his servants. Perhaps his first ambition had been to expel
the Romans from Asia; and when this had been achieved he
may have wished to sit quiet and defend his own frontiers. But
Rhodes had defied him; and Rhodes, so near to Asia, ruled
dominions on the mainland. Preparations were undertaken for
a siege of the hostile republic. The Pontic fleet, commanded by
Archelaus, sailed south from the Hellespont to cover these
operations.

Proceeding through the Cyclades Archelaus found the island
Greeks eager to be freed from their Roman masters. The
Romans had no fleet in the Aegean, and almost by accident
Archelaus became master of every island east of the Peloponnese. In particular he took by assault Delos, the great slave-
market; there, and in the neighbouring islands, he slew 20,000
Italian merchants. But Delos was much more than a slave-
market; its famous shrine of Apollo was traditionally under
Athenian protection, and it had formed part of the ancient
Athenian empire. Both Mithradates and Archelaus were loyal
servants of Delian Apollo; faced with the problem of safeguarding the treasures of his shrine in the midst of war they hit
on the solution of sending them to Athens.

The treasure was despatched in the care of a certain Aristion, an Athenian philosopher who had arrived in Pergamum as the envoy of the democratic faction in Athens. Soon after the money arrived Athens was swept by revolution; Aristion, now very much richer, led the democrats to overthrow the oligarchy installed by Rome. The new government offered Mithradates the alliance of free Athens and her newly restored empire.

This was a most astonishing turn of affairs. For more than a century Athens had been at peace and disarmed, declining in wealth and population, preserved from decay only by her repute as a centre of learning. No Roman had ever presumed to govern this museum of the arts, though her city council must of course follow the advice of the propraetor in Macedonia; no tribute was exacted from her, and no military contingent. For though it is likely that some Athenians adopted the popular calling of mercenary soldier, in the year 88 not even the oldest citizen had drilled in an Athenian phalanx or pulled at an oar in an Athenian warship. Athens had neither any grievance against the Romans who protected her, nor any military force with which to defend herself.

But eastward across the sea Greeks were making war on barbarians. The spirits of great ancestors, 400 years dead, filled once more the crowd in the assembly. Long ago the Athenian navy had supported Ionians rightly struggling to be free; once again Athens must be the champion of Hellas. With absurd and sublime devotion the city of Athens declared war on the city of Rome.

Even without army or navy Athens was still an ally of great value. Her prestige throughout the Greek world was immense, and in the Acropolis and the neighbouring seaport of Piraeus she controlled two of the strongest fortresses in Europe. As soon as Mithradates learned of these developments he sent his main army and the fleet, under the command of Archelaus, to garrison such valuable windfalls. Preparations continued for the siege of Rhodes; but for that another fleet, gathered from the Ionian cities, should suffice.

Where Athens set the example other Greeks must follow; the defections from Rome became a landslide. While Archelaus was safeguarding his communications by the occupation of Euboea he heard that Sparta, even more decayed than Athens, and Thebes, where some prosperity still lingered, had also joined the Pontic alliance. Two victories, over Nicomedes and Aquilius, had been sufficient to make Mithradates supreme over all Peloponnese, Attica and Boeotia, King from the Caucasus to the Adriatic.

Such was the loathing with which the civilized subjects of Rome regarded their masters.

Meanwhile Rhodes, isolated in a sea of enemies, remained faithful to the Roman cause. Cassius had found refuge there, with other fugitives from the great massacre; the citizens, undismayed, were strengthening their walls and building warships. They made war with dignity, as became true Greeks. Since they still made use of the public buildings erected at the expense of Mithradates they would not cast down the statue with which they had thanked him, and they gave quarter to Pontic prisoners. But they were determined on resistance to the last man. Mithradates in person sailed with the great armada gathered to destroy them; though he left the tactical command to his hired expert, Neoptolemus.

Protected by their fleet, the besiegers landed unmolested on the island. But though the Rhodian navy was not strong enough to fight a general action, Rhodian sailors were daring. Darting out from harbour, they inflicted more than one humiliating check on superior numbers of the enemy. During one of these combats six Rhodian cruisers, after a slow withdrawal, suddenly turned about to attack the twenty-five Pontic vessels which pursued them; they sank two ships and scattered the rest without loss to themselves. In this skirmish Mithradates suffered a misadventure which brought important consequences. He had gone out in his own ship to encourage his men, when in the heat of action an allied Chiot galley ran foul of him. Presumably his yacht was not rammed amidships, or he would have been in the water; but the collision was severe, and for a short time he was in personal danger.

To impute bad faith to an ally will break up any coalition; ostensibly Mithradates treated the mishap as an accident. But privately he was not so sure. After all, he had spent much of his youth avoiding assassination, and he still kept his bow handy even at meals. He knew that in every Greek city there was a Roman party, the displaced oligarchs. Only a few years ago the

Romans had bribed King Bocchus of Mauretania to betray King Jugurtha of Numidia into their hands; they might well bribe an allied sea-captain to murder him under cover of an accident. Presently he found excuses to punish, on other charges, the pilot of the Chiot ship and the sailor who had failed to keep a proper look-out. It was not long before the city of Chios felt his vengeance. But it went farther than that. Henceforth he feared treachery from every ally. It was the end of the honeymoon between the barbarian champion of freedom and the oppressed Greek cities.

Since his navy could not cope with Rhodian seamanship Mithradates summoned his whole army from the mainland. His transports encountered a storm, and at the height of the tempest Rhodian warships attacked them; but after heavy loss sufficient troops were landed to make possible an assault on the city from the inland. This assault was incompetently planned, perhaps by Mithradates himself; its combination of reckless haste and disregard of casualties does not suggest the professional mercenary. Under cover of darkness scaling ladders were to be reared against the wall, the attack to be synchronized with another assault on the harbour by a landing party from the fleet. No attempt had been made to breach the defences, or to construct works as cover for the approaches.

A Rhodian sentry spotted the escalading-party; the alarm-beacon he lit was mistaken by the navy for the signal of success. As a result both bodies of stormers were prematurely exposed, the defenders had ample time to man their wall, and neither assault was pushed home. Disheartened by the failure of his *coup de main*, Mithradates turned to orthodox siege-craft.

His engineers were set to building a marine siege-tower of exceptional size. The *sambuca* was a well-known device for the attack of shore defences, a tower and drawbridge mounted on a ship. Since the walls of Rhodes were uncommonly high, this particular sambuca must itself be built on a bridge between two of the largest ships in the Pontic fleet. When all was ready small boats, crowded with soldiers, began to tow the thing into position. But the engineers of antiquity never understood a fundamental limitation of their work: that the weight of a structure increases as the cube of its size, while the strength of its members increases only as the square of their breadth; they were

The Liberator of Hellas

often tempted to build bigger than their materials would allow. Strained by movement over moving water the sambuca collapsed, and the raft of precious timber that remained was set on fire by the missiles of the defenders. (The Rhodians themselves claimed that the goddess Isis had miraculously burned it in defence of her faithful city.)

After this misfortune Mithradates returned in disgust to Pergamum, and presently the siege dwindled to an inefficient blockade. The King's venture on the high seas had not been completely unrewarded. Many islands came over to his cause, of which Cos in particular was a valuable prize; for there he picked up a young grandson of the Queen-regent of Egypt and a great hoard of the treasure of the Ptolemies. The youth was brought up in all honour at the Pontic court, but his money went straight into the Pontic war-chest. Up to this point Mithradates had made a profit out of his war; while the troops were sure of their pay he could keep the loyalty of his new subjects by reducing their taxes. But in the south his fortunes had reached high tide. He had seen his soldiers on the walls of Rhodes, he would never see those walls from within.

In Europe also his armies had been checked. After securing the Peloponnese Archelaus advanced through Boeotia, where Thebes had declared for the King; only the little city of Thespiae stood firm for Rome, and he sat down to besiege it at leisure. At the same time the main Pontic fleet, commanded by a mercenary named Metrophanes, occupied Euboea and pushed cautiously up the east coast of Thessaly. Soon these combined forces would reach the southern boundary of Macedonia, whose Roman garrison would be caught between the army of Greek liberation and the barbarians pressing south from Haemus. To make quite sure of success another army had begun a long approach march. Arcathius, late King of Cappadocia, led a great host of Asiatic horse and foot which was to reach the eastern boundary of Macedonia by way of the Hellespont. These men had a very long way to go, and much of their journey lay through the uncivilized districts of Thrace, where they must forage for supplies and move very slowly; but by the summer of 87 Arcathius should link up with Archelaus.

The Romans in Macedonia were not dismayed; no Roman

The Liberator of Hellas

army was ever dismayed by great odds. The propraetor in command reacted to this converging attack after the classical method set down in every handbook of strategy. From his central position he struck out at the nearest hostile force, hoping to destroy it before the concentration was complete. The propraetor himself, with the bulk of his troops, must hold the northern margin of civilization against barbarian forays. But he sent southward an amphibious force, under his legate Bruttius Sura.

Bruttius won a sea-fight against the ships of Metrophanes, who thereupon retired inland to the centre of Euboea. Next the Romans swooped on Skiathos, the Pontic base, which was crammed with sick and plunder. Thousands of prisoners were taken. Those of free birth had their hands cut off before they were let loose to beg their way home, but the numerous runaway slaves were crucified. In Asia 80,000 Italians had been murdered; there would be no quarter in this war.

Bruttius then turned inland to Boeotia, where he skirmished with the great host of Archelaus. These encounters round Chaeronea were filled with echoes from the heroic past; for with the forces of Archelaus served the citizen-levies of Athens and Sparta, shadows of great armies long abolished. Once more, but for the last time, the paean of Marathon and Thermopylae was heard on the battlefield.

Bruttius held his own against superior numbers until a typically Roman piece of red tape compelled him to break off the campaign. He was informed that Sulla, commissioned by the Roman People to make war on Mithradates, claimed the sole right to conduct military operations in Boeotia; the army of Macedonia was trespassing, and must return to its province. Bruttius obeyed, and Archelaus overran Boeotia unopposed.

None the less, even as he obeyed Bruttius was able to draw the war southward, away from Macedonia. He retired to Piraeus, where he embarked his army. Archelaus, following him, settled down in Piraeus when the Romans sailed north to their province.

A small force of Romans had marched right through the Pontic front, from Chaeronea to Piraeus. Some Greek cities began to wonder whether they had really chosen the winning side. Aristion and his Athenian people's democracy were too thoroughly committed to turn back; but the famous little cities of the Peloponnese sent no contingents to later battles, and opened their gates at the approach of any army, whether Roman or Pontic.

Thus by January 87 there were already signs that the tide was on the turn. Mithradates, aged 44, ruled from the Euphrates to the Gulf of Corinth. He was popular with his new subjects; and Asia, freed from Roman oppression, was enjoying a brief phase of prosperity. But only once had the King himself appeared in arms, and then his forces had met with a humiliating reverse; Rhodes remained unsubdued, a Roman outpost within sight of the shore of Asia. In Greece a mere legate had shown that Roman soldiers could march through a Pontic army.

During the winter, while campaigning was suspended, the citizens of Pergamum devised a splendid masque in honour of the Liberator King. Mithradates sat enthroned in the royal box of the theatre as choirs sang his praises, and allegorical figures thanked him for benefits conferred. The climax of the festival was to be the descent from on high of a great image of Victory; the goddess bore a crown, to be deposited on the King's brow. It was the kind of empty pageant which the Greeks of the first century enjoyed staging in their theatres better than a performance of classical tragedy.

Something went wrong, as happened so often when Greek engineers tried to manage heavy weights. As Victory offered her crown the image broke loose and fell to the ground; the crown was also dashed to the ground and shattered, just as it approached the brow of Mithradates. All who saw were dismayed at the omen, and none more than Mithradates. He made inquiries, to find out whether at that moment one of his armies in Europe or Asia had suffered a check. He learned that nothing important had happened on that day; save that Sulla had sailed from Italy with an army of five legions.

Although Mithradates had not begun the war at a time of his own choosing, but had reacted to the unprovoked aggression of Aquilius, the year 88 was in fact a very good period in which to pluck feathers from the tail of the Roman Eagle. During that summer, for the first time in its history, the city of Rome fell to the assault of a Roman army. Sulla, one of the elected Consuls, had been driven from the city by the Popular mob. The Social War was not quite extinct, and he fled to the army which was engaged in besieging the rebel Italian city of Nola. For the first time the breach was revealed which had opened between the professional long-service legionary and the loafer in the Forum whose trade was selling his vote. The soldiers willingly followed Sulla to the capture of Rome. The Popular leader Marius fled into hiding.

Although Sulla was now legally and actually master of Rome he scrupled to interfere with the freedom of the annual elections. He was dismayed to see them won by the Populars; one of the new Consuls, who would take office in January 87, was his bitter enemy. He had a choice of two paths, and he chose without hesitation.

He might have kept his great army in Italy; he would have retained the power of the sword, and the Populars, whatever their elected majority, would not have dared to oppress the nobles. But then Roman dominion in the east would have been lost for ever. Though in Rome the bitterness of party strife had risen to unprecedented heights, and though by his absence he abandoned many of his supporters to death at the hands of the mob, Sulla led his legions to the Adriatic.

He took what precautions he might, though he must have known they would be in vain. Cinna, the new Consul, swore a weighty oath to live at peace with the nobility. Because civil war had emptied the treasury the temples were plundered of the offerings of past ages, so that the army was equipped with a great war-chest.

As soon as the army was oversea Cinna broke his promise; a decree of the people dismissed Sulla from his command, and he was proclaimed a public enemy. Throughout the struggle which followed he could draw no supplies from Rome, neither reinforcements nor money; and his men were not aristocratic volunteers, but professional soldiers who must be paid punctually. Because he so daringly left a revolution behind him he must live on the country from the moment he landed in Greece.

All the same, he brought to Thessaly five legions, 30,000 infantry of the line, a very great army. Pontic troops had not advanced beyond the Gulf of Corinth, and the northern Greeks were not committed to rebellion. In Thessaly and Aetolia Sulla was received as a friend, and in those parts he was able to enlist all the cavalry and light troops which a Roman general was expected to raise locally. Archelaus still lay in Piraeus, whither he had been drawn in pursuit of Bruttius. Frightened to see Sulla marching straight through Boeotia on Attica, Thebes deserted back to the Roman cause and the Peloponnesian cities protested their loyalty; all the Greek dominions of Mithradates melted away, save only Athens and her port of Piraeus. When Bruttius enticed Archelaus southward he had done much to win the war. The movement *looked* like a retreat, and that was enough to decide many waverers.

Seen from Pergamum the fighting was still very distant; a retreat from Boeotia into Attica was a mere tactical withdrawal. Mithradates recruited more troops, and for the first time imposed taxation on the cities of Asia. But it was only natural that he should send most of the available reinforcements to Arcathius, his son. When the young man lingered in Thrace, organizing the barbarians of those parts into a Kingdom of which he would of course be viceroy, his father did not order him to hurry. His junction with Archelaus, planned for 87, must now be postponed to the following year. But Athens and Piraeus were strong fortresses. Archelaus, whose forces outnumbered those of Sulla, should be able to maintain his position through another campaign.

It was perhaps about this time that Mithradates was distracted by a slight rearrangement of his domestic life. One evening a harper played before the court, accompanied by his daughter on the flute. The King was taken by the pretty face of Stratonice the flute-player, and after a whole year of Monime he was ready for a change. Next morning the strolling harper woke to find himself so rich that he rode shouting through the streets to proclaim his good fortune; at court Stratonice was supreme. Monime was packed off to a castle of inland Pontus where the King kept a herd of retired concubines.

In Attica Sulla settled down to siege-warfare. The Long Walls built by Themistocles between Athens and Piraeus were now in ruins, and Athens could be completely blockaded. The city was in the hands of convinced revolutionaries, willing to fight to the last man for freedom and Mithradates. But Aristion, their leader, was no soldier. Before the war he had been a professional philosopher; Appian remarks that such men always make bad rulers. Attica is a barren region, and it may not have been any-one's fault that the city was already short of food when the Romans closed round it. But Aristion's idea of fair shares was not equal shares; while most of the citizens went hungry he revelled with his friends on the Acropolis.

The fame of Athens made it an important prize; but it was defended only by its citizen militia, who would never dare to meet Roman legionaries in the field. The focus of the campaign was Piraeus, in which lay Archelaus and the main Pontic army. His position was immensely strong. The landward walls of Piraeus had been built by Pericles; since Sulla did not com-mand a single warship the Asiatics could draw unlimited sup-plies and reinforcements from oversea; in numbers, especially in cavalry, they were superior to their besiegers. But man for man their infantry were not the equals of Roman foot, and Archelaus was reluctant to offer battle in the open.

The chief difficulties which Sulla must overcome were those of supply. In barren Attica he could find no food, and he dared not weaken his army by sending detachments to forage afield. Merchants would bring him corn if he could pay for it; but the money he had with him would not last for ever, and a declared public enemy could expect no more from Rome. Relying on the prestige of Roman arms he sent envoys to the priestly colleges in Epidaurus, Olympia, and Delphi, the richest shrines in Greece. With sardonic wit he pointed out that the times were disturbed, and that their treasuries might be pillaged by ban-dits; their wealth would be safe only in the Roman camp. Reluctantly the priests took the hint. Even the offering of King Croesus of Lydia, which had stood in Delphi for 500 years, was sent to pay the army which was quenching the last embers of Greek freedom.

Timber also was lacking. At that time an army seldom car-ried its siege-engines on the march; usually the machines were made where they were needed. But in all Attica there were no tall trees, save in the sacred and famous grove of Academe, just under the walls of Athens. So Academe was felled, the nursery of philosophy. Amid the lamentations of the Athenians Roman catapults were built to pound the Periclean walls of Piraeus.

All through the summer siege operations continued. Daily 20,000 mules brought up missiles and supplies for the Roman engineers; the ruins of the Long Walls were grubbed up to make a tall mound. But a premature escalade was repelled with heavy loss; and Archelaus, with the open sea at his back, could bring in reinforcements from the Cyclades as he needed them. Sulla just maintained his position, because Roman sympathizers in the Pontic camp sent him news of the enemy's movements scratched on the lead balls which were shot by the catapults. He could anticipate every Pontic sortie, and on one occasion repelled an attack with such vigour that Archelaus himself was shut out from his own gate and had to be pulled up the wall by a rope.

Yet the Roman army was cut off from home, while every day Archelaus grew stronger. Sulla saw that he could not win without a fleet. In the autumn he sent a favourite lieutenant, Lucullus, to enlist one. In a fast sailing-ship, which could keep the open sea better than any galley, Lucullus dodged the Pontic cruisers. It was learned that he had reached Egypt in safety. Then there was no more news of him.

Winter came with the deadlock unbroken. Archelaus could not drive off his besiegers, but neither could he be driven from Piraeus. Athens, though very hungry, still held out. Sulla dared not work his men too hard. In law he was a criminal, with no right to command; they obeyed him only from respect and affection. Reluctantly he withdrew to winter quarters in Eleusis, though a detachment still kept up the blockade of Athens.

In January 86 Mithradates, aged 45, had been reigning splendidly in Pergamum for more than a year. Despite the setback in Attica his dominions were more extensive than ever before, for Arcathius had now conquered much of Roman Macedonia. But his Ionian subjects were growing discontented. His armies needed constant reinforcement, and for lack of volunteers he must resort to compulsory service. This the peaceful Greeks of Asia thought incompatible with liberty, though to their ancestors service in arms had been the mark of the free man. Heavy taxes were now needed to pay for the long war.

The secret police were active. The King had never forgotten that regrettable incident with the Chiot ship, and any rumour of disaffection led to arrests and torture. But the principal ground of Ionian discontent was one of the original planks in the platform of liberation. The enfranchisement of resident aliens annoyed even extreme democrats, as jealous of anyone outside their closed community as the members of a modern Trade Union. Yet such was the will of the King in Pergamum, which could be upset only by calling back the Romans.

Early in the new year Sulla returned to his trenches before Piraeus. During the long blockade a few convoys had slipped into Athens, only four miles from the main Pontic position. But the city was at the point of starvation; the sacred lamp before the Maiden Goddess went out for lack of oil, and there were rumours of cannibalism. It seems odd that Sulla, who fought so fiercely at Piraeus, never ordered an escalade at Athens. Perhaps his soldiers were frightened of the fame of its magnificent defences, even though these were held by a handful of starving civilians.

On the 1st of March in the second year of the siege the long agony of Athens was ended, more or less by accident. Roman pickets at a listening-post under the wall overheard discontented citizens grumbling that Aristion neglected his duty; while he sat idle on the Acropolis a section of the lower town-wall had fallen into ruin. When this was reported to Sulla he ordered an assault that very night. Once over the ruined wall the Romans carried all before them. But a successful escalade in the dark was bound to end in a bloody massacre; by dawn the stream of blood trickled beneath a gate into the open country. Sulla stopped the slaughter while enough Athenians were still alive to ensure the continuance of the city. But the Roman army, which must make war support war for so long as the Populars held power in the Forum, stripped them of all their property. The temple of the Maiden was pillaged, and every slave in the town was sold for the benefit of the Roman war-chest.

For a few days Aristion and his bodyguard held out on the Acropolis; thirst compelled him to yield. In this contemporaries saw the judgment of heaven on a tyrannous philosopher. In

March the cisterns of the Acropolis should have been brimming; drought had emptied them and no rain fell—until the evening after the surrender, when it poured.

The fate of Aristion is uncertain; some say he was killed at once, others that he was reserved as an ornament for Sulla's Triumph. This last seems more probable, as the usual fate of an enemy commander. But there is no doubt that he did not live to see Rome.

The capture of Athens and the dreadful punishment of its defenders won great fame for Sulla and his army. Henceforth the Greeks of Europe dared not oppose Romans. But seen in perspective, as perhaps it was seen in Asia, the military lesson of the campaign was not wholly favourable to the Romans. They had been held up for a year and a half by very strong walls, manned by untrained civilians. The cities of Ionia were just as lavishly fortified as Athens, and their citizens could see that a fight to the death might be better than submission to Roman vengeance.

In fact Sulla was very awkwardly placed. While Athens still held out he had been joined by his wife and children, barely escaped with their lives from the terror organized by the Populars in Rome; other noble fugitives continually straggled into his camp, with stories of mass-executions and confiscations of property. They begged him to break off the Greek campaign and lead his troops against their domestic enemies. But his soldiers, though they liked him, were not partisans of aristocracy; they followed a great general so long as he provided them with plunder. While no money reached him from Italy he must lead them from victory to victory. He decided to expel the invaders from Europe before he returned to restore order in Rome.

There was no time to be lost. The Pontic army in Macedonia was at last moving south. During the autumn it had remained halted while Arcathius organized his new Kingdom, and in the early spring its young commander fell sick and could not travel. Now he was dead; the new general was Taxiles, a tough mercenary who fought battles without wasting time in organizing Kingdoms. Piraeus must be taken before Taxiles could join Archelaus, or the Roman army would be outmatched.

There was fierce fighting before the landward walls of Piraeus. Sulla heaped up a great mound to overtop the defences, Archelaus undermined it, Sulla dug countermines, savage battles were fought underground. When even the masonry of Pericles could not stand up to the incessant pounding Archelaus built another wall behind the tottering breach, and another behind that when it in its turn was battered. But such a struggle could have only one end, for after a few unfortunate sorties Archelaus clung to the defensive. He feared to commit his unwieldy phalanx to a battle of manœuvre against fast-moving legionary swordsmen, and among the trenches and mounds of the siege-works his superior cavalry could not charge. Thus when the Romans were checked they still clung to their front-line trenches, but each time Archelaus was repulsed he must yield another segment of the town.

As the result of many little retreats Archelaus presently found himself cramped for room. Since the Romans had no fleet his communications with Asia were unmolested, and after the fall of Athens there were no longer reasons of prestige for clinging to the ruins of Piraeus. Taxiles was advancing to join him, but that did not compel him to wait; the Pontic armies could be united just as well in Boeotia as in Attica. Accordingly he withdrew his men by detachments, and sent them round by sea to join Taxiles in the neighbourhood of Thermopylae; his rearguard held on to Munychia, the citadel of Piraeus, until most skilfully he slipped away, taking with him his sick, his stores, and his war-chest. The Romans surged into battered Piraeus, and in their advance destroyed the famous harbour installations of Pericles and Themistocles. But their conquest was only in the technical sense a victory.

Archelaus was a tactician of the first class. He had carried out with complete success one of the most difficult operations of war, an embarkation in the face of the enemy. Furthermore, he judged accurately the capacity of his troops. Behind walls or entrenchments the spearmen of Asia, as brave individually as any Roman, could fight with good prospects; in open ground the nimble swordsmen of the legions would probably break them in flank. Therefore for as long as he could he fought behind walls, and when he retired he moved right away from hilly Attica to the Boeotian plain, where his cavalry could charge unhampered. Two years of warfare had stripped Attica of all supplies; he could expect that Sulla, marching north by land, would bring a starved army to meet him.

After his junction with Taxiles Archelaus led 100,000 foot and 20,000 horse to the border of Boeotia and Phocis. There he encountered Sulla with 30,000 legionaries and a few hundred mercenary horse. Archelaus repeatedly offered battle; but Sulla remained in his palisaded camp, where it would be suicide to attack him. As a rule Sulla was eager for battle, but for once his men had taken fright at the overwhelming number of the enemy. Presently Archelaus understood that he could not compel trained Roman soldiers to fight against their will. He marched past their camp, and continued eastward to get in touch with his fleet at Chalcis in Euboea.

The legionaries recovered their nerves as suddenly as they had lost them; and the Pontic army had now left the open plain for a region of rocky hills where cavalry could not deploy. Sulla, marching in pursuit, found Archelaus halted in a badly sited camp near the city of Chaeronea, which was held by a Roman garrison. Archelaus, with 20,000 troop horses to feed, could not sit tight behind his palisade; and local guides showed the Romans a path to the top of a steep hill from whence they could roll down boulders among the Pontic tents. Archelaus was forced to come out and fight just the kind of battle that did not suit his army; a head-on clash between phalanx and legion, with no room for sweeping cavalry charges.

He tried again the novel weapon which two years ago had destroyed the Bithynians. It seems likely that he had little faith in it, since he had never before used it against Romans. He had with him sixty war-chariots, and in the cramped valley which was the battlefield the legions might not have room to dodge them. At the beginning of the action they were launched against the enemy line.

A tactical novelty never dismayed the Romans. Since by definition Roman tactics were the best anything strange must be inferior. The legions merely opened their ranks before the charge, and the chariots swept through. As the drivers pulled up for another try they were surrounded by the Roman reserve and the horses shot down with javelins. The imperturbable legionaries then shouted for more chariots, as though they were sitting in the Roman Circus impatient for the next race to begin.

But the Romans grew really angry when they discovered that the Pontic phalanx was composed of 15,000 freed slaves. A centurion cried reproachfully: 'This isn't the Saturnalia!'—the one day in the year on which slaves were allowed to bother their betters.

Then a charge of Pontic horse pierced the Roman front; but the two halves of the line fought on, and Sulla in person led his handful of cavalry in a counter-charge which eased the pressure. The phalanx advanced in support; but after heavy fighting the legions broke it in flank. Archelaus tried to halt the retreat by shutting the gates of his camp; the fugitives burst in, with the Romans following. Once the camp was lost the whole army dissolved in flight. Archelaus reached his base at Chalcis, across the Euripus, with 10,000 survivors out of the 120,000 men whom he had led into battle. Sulla put the loss of the Roman army at thirteen men in all, but his estimate was not generally believed.

Behind the Euripus Archelaus was safe. With great resolution he still made a front against Sulla, sending sea-borne detachments to raid the harbours of the mainland. Facing him, Sulla garrisoned the eastern coast of Boeotia. Both armies settled down to pass the winter.

When he was told about the battle Mithradates was amazed. He had never seen war, and he could not understand how 30,000 men could defeat four times their own number. There must have been treachery somewhere; he looked round for a scapegoat.

It is to his credit that he did not dismiss Archelaus, an honest mercenary who gave value for money, a good soldier who had the misfortune to encounter a general of genius. Instead he raised another army; Dorylaus, son of his father's old general, would take it to Euboea and there hand over to Archelaus. But if the high command was sound there must have been traitors in the ranks; they would be hunted down.

The Galatians had a reputation for treachery, so he began by teaching them a lesson. He invited their chieftains to a state banquet, and there had them murdered, with their wives and children. Even these firm measures did not make them loyal. Three chieftains who had escaped from the massacre raised an army of fierce Gallic tribesmen. The urgent need to reinforce Euboea had weakened the Pontic garrisons in Asia; soon the last soldiers of Mithradates were expelled from Galatia; which returned to the condition of liberty, or rather anarchy, congenial to the Celtic temperament.

Chios, the wicked city whose sailors had once rammed the King's own yacht, was probably another nest of traitors. A fate was planned for it which must strike terror into all waverers. Quietly the town was occupied by a strong force of mercenaries, ostensibly on the march to reinforce Archelaus. Zenobius, their commander, then accused the citizens of stealing the confiscated property of murdered Italians, instead of handing it over to the King's treasury; as punishment for this fraud he imposed on them a fine of 2,000 talents. The unfortunate Chiots tried to raise the money, in the middle of a war which had closed all the trade-routes; they stripped all the temples and public buildings in their city. Zenobius declared that the miscellaneous heap of gold, silver and bronze was not nearly enough. As defaulters, the whole body of citizens were sent in chains to Mithradates at Pergamum. The King sentenced them to be transported to the Euxine, the men separately from the women and children, so that their community would be extinguished. It is said that the ships carrying them to Colchis were attacked by the men of Heraclea, and the captives set free; certainly the city of Chios existed after this war was finished. But for a time it was left desolate.

The atrocity failed of its effect. Zenobius marched next to Ephesus; where the citizens, fearing the fate of Chios, would not permit him to bring his troops within the walls. Rashly he entered alone, to confer with Philopoemen the father of Monime, whom Mithradates had appointed as governor. The Ephesians killed him, closed their gates, and declared for Rome. Philopoemen disappears from history; he may have joined the revolt against a King who had grown tired of his beautiful daughter, or he may have been lynched by angry citizens. The example of Ephesus was followed by Tralles and other towns.

Mithradates could not spare troops to subdue these rebels. Instead he did them what harm he could by political measures. In a proclamation he decreed that in these cities all slaves, as well as resident foreigners, were henceforth enfranchized citizens. The result was as he had foreseen. For the next few years bloody civil conflicts paralysed the cities of Ionia, as slaves fought for the right conferred on them by the Liberator King, and the old citizens fought to preserve their privileges.

Even Pergamum was tainted with disloyalty. Four Greeks among the King's most intimate friends plotted his assassination; then one of the plotters informed on the other three. It is impossible to disentangle the motives for these palace-plots, or to discover why Asclepiodotus of Lesbos first planned murder and then turned informer. But once the King's secret police had begun their inquiries they naturally, like secret police everywhere, unmasked many more suspects. First eighty Pergamenes were arrested; after they had been tortured some 1,600 Greeks, from all the cities of Asia, were seized and put to death. Informers were lavishly rewarded; thereafter they must serve the King faithfully, in fear of Roman vengeance.

During the same autumn Mithradates discovered that the Romans had enlisted a war-fleet, though the news did not cross the sea to Sulla. The King of Egypt, though he feared to take an open part in the war, had given a great sum of money to Lucullus, who with it hired ships from the harbours of Syria. He had broken the blockade outside Rhodes, picked up the excellent little Rhodian navy, and was now working his way northward in the direction of Chios and the Hellespont.

In January 85 Mithradates still ruled in Pergamum; but his power was declining. Galatia was lost, and much of Ionia. The Cyclades were being nibbled away by Lucullus; Euboea was the only Pontic foothold left in Europe. Archelaus would be reinforced in the spring, and if he beat Sulla all might be regained; but that was the very last chance. So far Mithradates, now aged 46, had behaved like any other palace-bred oriental despot. He was a competent administrator with a head for figures; he could keep his treasury solvent and arrange the pay and supplies of the large armies he enlisted. But by his bloody tyranny he had thrown away the devotion once felt by the Greeks for their deliverer from Roman oppression. Except for the war-chariots, which had proved a failure, he had thought of no new tactical device; and he left to hired experts the command of his troops in the field. Another defeat for his army, and the non-combatant King would be finished for ever. No one would have prophesied, during those last shaky months of Pontic rule in Pergamum, that more than twenty years later Mithradates would still be a foe feared by the bravest Roman.

As 85 opened Sulla also had his worries. His domestic enemies, who controlled Rome, were now taking a hand in the foreign war. Flaccus, one of the Popular Consuls for the year 86, landed in Illyria with two legions. Ostensibly he came to fight Mithradates, but to every Popular Sulla was a greater danger.

Yet Flaccus, a politician with little military experience, was not eager to attack the victors of Chaeronea. When he reached northern Thessaly he continued towards Macedonia, as though to march by Thrace and the Hellespont to the invasion of the Pontic possessions in Asia. Sulla, not wishing to lose touch with this army of potential enemies, withdrew northward from Boeotia to follow his march.

About the same time Dorylaus reached Euboea with 80,000 reinforcements, bringing up the strength of the Pontic field-army to nearly 100,000 men. The enthusiasts for Greek liberty, especially the phalanx of freed slaves, had been wiped out at Chaeronea; the foot of this second army was composed of inferior material. But the horse were Pontic barons and their households, the best cavalry in the world and devoted to their King.

Archelaus was always quick to see an opening; as soon as Sulla withdrew from his front he recrossed the Euripus and reoccupied Boeotia. Most rashly, the Thebans welcomed him a second time. When they surrendered after Chaeronea Sulla had spared their lives, but he had not spared their purses. He was as superstitious as he was ruthless, and his pillaging of the Greek shrines weighed on his conscience. He made amends to Apollo by assigning the public revenue of Thebes to pay off his sacrilegious debt by instalments.

To meet the new threat Sulla faced southward. On the edge of the Copaic marshes, at Orchomenus, only a few miles from Chaeronea, he offered battle in a prepared position. His men were drawn up in an open plain, which looked ideal for cavalry; but he had entrenched his front, and strewed caltrops before his line. Archelaus had to attack him. A Pontic commander could not assume that the rival Roman armies would never act in concert; his only chance was to crush Sulla quickly, before Flaccus came south to join him.

Archelaus very nearly won the vital battle. Before the charge of the Pontic horse the legions recoiled. Sulla was just able to restore the situation by appealing, not to the patriotism of his men, but to their professional pride. Before his wavering line he dismounted, alone save for his orderlies. Turning, he shouted: 'Soldiers, when you are asked where you abandoned your leader, say it was at Orchomenus.'

After a long struggle, in which the son of Archelaus was killed, the Pontic cavalry were fought to a standstill. By evening they had lost 10,000 men, more than half of their total number; and 5,000 of the less useful foot had also fallen. Archelaus withdrew to his palisaded camp, which was protected by the marsh in its rear. But as dusk fell Sulla advanced, and dug in within long arrow-range.

Early next morning the Romans stormed the camp of the disheartened barbarians; the fugitives were driven into the marsh to drown. For a few days Archelaus was himself missing, believed killed; alone he got through the marsh in a small boat, and alone he reached Calchis.

There was now no Pontic army. Out of the 180,000 men whom Mithradates had sent to Europe, only a few stragglers returned. The war was lost. But diplomacy might still save something out of the wreck, if the two Roman armies chose to continue their domestic civil war on the frontiers of Asia.

Sulla had no ships, and he was still without news of Lucullus. He could not invade Asia unless he marched to the Propontis, where he must collide with Flaccus. The latter was not a good soldier, but now he had no enemy to beat; he advanced unopposed as far as Byzantium and prepared to cross the Bosphorus. Mithradates, with his palace-guard and the scrapings of his depots, still clung to Pergamum; though Flaccus was now in a position to cut him off from Pontus.

The Ionian cities thought only of making terms with Rome; but the most humble surrender brought no safety. Flaccus threatened that if they yielded to Sulla he would treat them as enemies, Sulla proclaimed that the friends of Flaccus must be his foes. At the same time extreme democrats, freed slaves, and informers who had worked with the secret police, all clamoured for further resistance.

After some preliminary negotiation about safe-conducts Archelaus arrived in Sulla's camp on the Boeotian shore of the Euripus. Ostensibly he had come to conclude an armistice, but each general took the opportunity to try to buy the other from his allegiance. Archelaus proposed that Sulla should stop the war with Asia still in Pontic hands; in return Mithradates would supply him with ships and money for his struggle against the Populars who controlled Rome. Sulla countered by offering to make Archelaus King of Pontus if he would desert his paymaster and bring his mercenaries into Roman service. Each general then expressed himself horrified at the other's treasonable proposal, and they settled down to hammer out a peace which would be fair to all parties.

Sulla could have chased Mithradates to the edge of the civilized world and beyond. But for the last two years the Populars had been murdering his friends, and he was anxious to get home and install an aristocratic government. If he restored the frontiers of 89 he could call himself victorious, and with a clear conscience return to Rome. It was agreed that Mithradates should hand over his warships as an acknowledgement of defeat, and retire from all his recent conquests; Nicomedes and Ariobarzanes would return to Bithynia and Cappadocia, and the Roman officials to the province of Asia. Final terms, including the amount of the indemnity to be paid by the loser, were left to be fixed at a personal interview between Sulla and the King. In the meantime there should be no more fighting.

Archelaus had served his employer with complete fidelity, in spite of considerable temptation. For three years he had withstood the Romans in hard-fought campaigns; now that his last army had perished he negotiated a very favourable armistice. But he was a soldier of fortune, not a patriot sworn to die for Pontus. He considered that the armistice released him from any further obligation to Mithradates. Henceforth he accompanied Sulla on his march to the Hellespont. He won the friendship of his old antagonist, who when he fell sick sent him his personal physician and halted the march of the Roman army to await his recovery. In the course of Sulla's settlement of the tangled affairs of mainland Greece, Archelaus received a great landed estate in Euboea; some say that Aristion, whose tyrannous government of Athens was held to have weakened the Pontic cause, was executed in Thrace to please him.

Meanwhile Flaccus began to lead his army over the Bosphorus; but while he was detained at Chalcedon on the Asiatic shore his chief lieutenant, Fimbria, organized a mutiny among the troops still at Byzantium in Europe. Flaccus fled shamefully from his own men to seek refuge in Nicomedia, whose citizens, in terror of Roman vengeance, opened their gates to the stray Roman officer. Fimbria and the mutineers pursued him. He was taken and killed while the frightened Greeks stood by without offering to help either side.

As Sulla marched north Fimbria in his turn was cut off from Rome. To keep the allegiance of his mutinous followers he must give them plunder, and the army which Mithradates had scraped together to defend his palace was not very formidable. Fimbria marched boldly against Pergamum, scattered the King's levies at the combat of Miletopolis, and threatened the capital itself. Its walls were strong, but Mithradates feared that the citizens might sell him to the Romans. Since Fimbria's army blocked the overland route to Pontus he fled to Pitane on the coast opposite Mytilene. There he unexpectedly found himself cornered, with Fimbria's soldiers at the landward gate and the ships of Lucullus, arrived at last on the scene of operations, crusing at the mouth of the harbour. Luckily for Mithradates Lucullus, who was always faithful to Sulla, considered Fimbria his most dangerous enemy. He proclaimed that the fleet was bound by the armistice concluded between his own commander and Archelaus. His ships remained idle while the King escaped to Mytilene.

At Dardanus in the Troad Mithradates at last met his conqueror. Pride drove him to demonstrate that he still led an army; he came to the conference at the head of 20,000 foot, 6,000 horse, and a number of the useless but showy scythed chariots. Sulla brought an escort of 200 horse and four cohorts of legionaries, perhaps 2,000 men in all; but at need they could have destroyed the mob of half-trained Pontic recruits. In Sulla's train were the Kings Nicomedes and Ariobarzanes, helpless lay figures to be pushed on or off thrones at the will of stronger men. After lengthy speeches of self-justification Sulla and Mithradates reached complete agreement, for at that particular moment both were in urgent need of peace. The King knew that if the war continued he might be driven even from the lands of his ancestors, Sulla was anxious to get his army on the march for Rome before the last of his friends were murdered by the Populars. Mithradates promised to evacuate even Paphlagonia, the only one of his conquests he had hoped to retain. The indemnity he must pay was fixed at the enormous sum of 2,000 talents; and he publicly went through the form of a reconciliation with his colleagues, the Kings of Bithynia and Cappadocia.

He promised also to hand over all deserters from the Roman forces, and all the renegades and freed slaves in his army. This promise was not kept, and it seems that Sulla did not expect it to be kept. With elaborate ceremonial peace was proclaimed. The struggle later known as the First Mithradatic War was terminated.

Eighty thousand murdered Italians were still unavenged, and Mithradates knew very well that the massacre would never be forgiven. The Peace of Dardanus was only a truce, which would be broken as soon as the Romans had finished their own more pressing civil war. Presently he would have to defend his homeland of Pontus, and his life. He went back to Sinope to get ready for the next war.

During 84 the Roman province of Asia suffered indescribable hardship. Every city was disturbed by the incompatible claims of refugees returning under Roman protection and immigrants enfranchized by Mithradates. During the war trade had been at a standstill, and public property had been sold to equip soldiers and repair fortifications. Sulla took credit for imposing no indemnity on penniless communities which could plead that they had been compelled by force to serve the King. Instead he pointed out to the repentent subjects of Rome that no tribute had reached the lawful authorities during the last five years; the whole sum must be paid to him as soon as possible. Until it had been paid he quartered his soldiers on prosperous householders, chosen because they had supported the King; these unwilling hosts must provide not only lodging for their guests, but also rations, pay, and even clothing.

The Liberator of Hellas

The soldiers of Fimbria also lived at free quarters among the unhappy Greeks. Fimbria denounced, as rebels against the legitimate government of Rome, all those cities which had offered submission to Sulla the public enemy. In punishment for this rebellion he exacted heavy contributions; and in default of payment utterly destroyed the city of Ilium, successor to Homeric Troy. (But the damage archaeologists deplore was not done by a foe, Roman or Achaean; the engineers of Augustus, rebuilding at his orders the home of his ancestors, planed away the last remains of the city of Priam to make a level foundation.)

Sulla's protection was expensive, but it was also effective. He soon took measures to quell Fimbria, who entrenched his camp and stood on the defensive. The Popular legions dared not meet in battle the victors of Chaeronea and Orchomenus; when an attempt to procure the assassination of Sulla had failed because of the obvious terror of the chosen murderer Fimbria could only beg terms of surrender. Sulla did not bother to meet him, but contemptuously sent word that his life would be spared if he went back to Rome at once and alone. Fimbria answered, with the flash of pride that might flare up unaccountably in the most scoundrelly Roman, that he knew of a quicker way home. In the chief temple of Pergamum he stabbed himself with his sword.

The Fimbrian legions submitted to Sulla. He would not bring declared Populars back to Rome, and therefore ordered them to remain behind as the garrison of Asia, under the command of his legate, Murena. But to help in the campaign against the Populars he took the surrendered ships of Mithradates. In all the Levant the only remaining navy was the squadron of war-torn Rhodes.

The pirates of Cilicia rose to new heights of audacity. They raided Samothrace while Sulla was actually visiting its shrines, and took more than a thousand talents of silver from the holy island. No harbour was safe from their blackmail. Pillaged Asia suffered an economic decline which lasted for centuries. Not until a Christian Emperor ruled in Constantinople did the cities of Ionia recover the prosperity they had known in 89 B.C.

III

The Statesman

In January 83 the King of Pontus, aged 48, seemed a spent
force. While the Romans were occupied with civil war he
had overrun most of Asia and Greece; but as soon as a
Roman army came against him he had been defeated utterly.
Not only had he failed, he had failed ingloriously. Only twice
had he seen action, and each time his personal tenure of command had been the occasion of defeat. The resources of his
great empire should have overcome the single city of Rhodes;
his nervous impatience had led to the repulse of a premature
assault. At Miletopolis he fought with second-rate troops; but
so indeed did Fimbria, who defeated him with contemptuous
ease. As a ruler he was efficient, and he had a flair for choosing
good servants and getting the best out of them. But the lesson of
his long reign of twenty-five years was clearly that he should
keep away from war.

On the other hand, it was unlikely that the Romans would
allow him to end his days in peace. Eighty thousand slaughtered
Italians were still unavenged. Whichever Roman army won the
civil war would come east to finish him off. Even if they did not,
an oriental despot cannot sit down quietly under the stigma of
defeat. Bosporus and Colchis were already restive. Mithradates
must prove that he still possessed the power of the sword.

Therefore as soon as he had surrendered his ships to Sulla he
began to gather another fleet, and to recruit his army. In military affairs he had learned by experience. He did not start to
train another phalanx; even desperate slaves, fighting for personal liberty, could not face Roman legions in that clumsy formation. Instead he drilled his foot in small units, easy to handle.
The spear was still their weapon, for he could not change at
short notice the immemorial habits of Asia; but they were

drawn up loosely, in thin lines, in the hope that they would fence as individuals against the individual Roman swordsmen. The proportion of light infantry was increased, for in his Armenian bowmen he had long-range skirmishers (their arrows killed at 200 yards) whom the javelin-throwing Romans could not match. But the heart of this new model army was the cavalry. The Persian nobles of inland Pontus followed their hereditary lord with chivalrous devotion. They could ride over their native mountains where strangers must go on foot; and they were not afraid to charge unbroken infantry.

The new forces were first employed against the rebels of Colchis. There the natives had declared for independence as soon as they heard that their overlord had concluded a shameful peace with Rome. They submitted to the threat of force, and were mollified when the King sent to them as governor his eldest son, another Mithradates. But young Mithradates, when he had a realm of his own, quickly developed a personal policy. Sensible client-Kings who surrendered their independence received in return peace and an ample revenue guaranteed by Rome; the cadets of Pontus must have been perpetually worried by the restless and dangerous schemes of the head of the family.

The young viceroy was recalled to Sinope, ostensibly for consultations. At the palace he was arrested, though in deference to his rank he was bound with golden fetters. Shortly afterwards he was executed as a traitor. The King had chosen the surname of Eupator, the Good Father; but sometimes events were too strong for his goodness.

In Bosporus the Greek cities remained loyal to their protector; but the barbarians of the steppe naturally began to raid the farmland as soon as they heard of his defeat. A strong expeditionary force was needed to restore order; it was led by the last surviving and youngest son of Mithradates and Laodice, a prince named Machares. When he had quelled the rebellion he remained in Bosporus as viceroy.

On the whole the intelligence and vigour of the three sons of Mithradates and his sister-Queen were above the average for Hellenistic royalty. The younger Mithradates had done well in the unfortunate campaign against Fimbria; in Thrace Arcathius had shown himself to be a competent soldier; Machares proved an efficient ruler of Bosporus. But it was only natural that the children of such parents should be wanting in filial piety. Posterity must remain ignorant of the King's long-term plans; it is not likely that he ever worked consciously for the heir who would come after him, as did for example some rulers of mediaeval France. In fact whether he had an aim other than personal hatred of Rome is uncertain.

These military operations on the shores of the Euxine alarmed some observers in the Roman province. They did not alarm Murena, but for other reasons he was eager for war. The greatest honour that could be granted to a Roman commander was a Triumph, a solemn procession of thanksgiving in which he led his army to the chief temple of the City. The honour was conferred by a solemn decree of the Senate, and afterwards enrolled among the official records; it would be remembered by the descendants of the hero for as long as the City should endure.

During the last century of the republic Triumphs were earned very easily; a skirmish with a band of brigands was enough to give the unwarlike Cicero a claim to the great honour, and the action of the Senate was often the result of a complicated political deal. But certain conditions must be fulfilled. The Triumphator must have been the genuine and official military commander, the magistrate in charge of the province; if the victory had been won by a subordinate, even if he commanded a detached force of troops, the glory went to the superior in whose name he had acted. The foe should by rights be foreigners, not the rival faction in a civil war or subjects risen in rebellion; though this condition was not always observed if the Senate had other reasons for gratifying the general.

At Chaeronea and Orchomenus Murena had distinguished himself as a corps commander; in Greece he had led a detached force of all arms, which had defeated detachments of the Pontic army. But the credit for these successes accrued to Sulla, the supreme commander. The government of Asia was Murena's first independent command. Furthermore, the chance was not likely to recur. He was Sulla's legate, appointed to govern the reconquered territories until the Populars should have been expelled from Rome. But he had no political record, and it would be many years before he was important enough to be elected praetor or Consul, and sent to rule abroad after serving his year of office in Rome.

If only there could be a war in Asia, before Sulla sent out a propraetor to replace him!

It was not hard to find an occasion for war. Mithradates was rearming, of that there could be no doubt. Murena himself was aware that the new army was being raised to fight the rebels in Bosporus; but that was not known to the general public, and he could produce reputable advisers who had warned him of approaching danger.

One of these advisers ought to be in a position to know the facts. Archelaus, late Pontic commander in Europe, fled suddenly from Sinope to seek asylum in Pergamum. He averred that Mithradates was planning a surprise attack on Roman territory, and that he had escaped because he feared to be implicated in a war that must end in disaster. That was not the real reason for his flight. He had changed sides because his employer no longer trusted him. Jealous courtiers had been reminding the King that his general had very quickly made friends with the Roman leader, from the moment negotiations were officially opened; Sulla had given him a valuable estate, safely on the Roman side of the frontier. Perhaps that interview after Orchomenus had not in fact been the first? Perhaps Archelaus had all the time been playing a double game? Mithradates could not make up his mind. But he did not offer Archelaus another command, and the mercenary feared that soon he might be arrested and interrogated.

No soldier of fortune could publish such a discreditable excuse for his desertion. It sounded much better if he said he had changed sides because Mithradates was about to break the treaty of peace.

The terms of that treaty had not been carried out in every particular, though the failure was not really the fault of the King of Pontus. It had been agreed that he should restore to King Ariobarzanes the whole of Cappadocia, as it had been in 89. But when it came to the point the nobles of central Cappadocia would not obey the puppet set over them by Rome; they had not obeyed him in the past, and they preferred to be ruled by a forceful and ambitious statesman of their own Persian stock. South of the old frontier of Pontus the chieftains of some inland valleys still counted themselves subjects of Mithradates. Ariobarzanes complained to his Roman protectors.

For all these reasons Murena considered that an attack on Pontus could be justified before the Senate in Rome. If he gained a single technical victory he would be qualified for a Triumph; and in any case he could gather enough plunder to keep the unruly Fimbrian legions obedient and contented. In the summer of 83, without waiting for a declaration of war, he led his army over the Cappadocian mountains to descend into the valley of the upper Lycus. He pillaged the holy and wealthy temple of Ma at Comana, and many other villages besides. (Comana ranked as a village because it had neither a municipality nor walls; though it was the home of, among others, 6,000 farmers and their families.)

Mithradates was taken by surprise. His new army was not ready for war, and the better part of it was on the far side of the Euxine. Besides, Sulla was still leading his veterans through Italy towards Rome, and if he chose to turn back he could destroy Pontus. When Murena had gathered enough plunder to content his legions he would probably go back across the frontier, and later he might be disavowed by the Senate; but if more Roman soldiers were killed by the King who had already murdered 80,000 Italians Rome would cry out for revenge.

Therefore Mithradates held back his troops from contact with the enemy. He did no more than send envoys to Murena, to claim the protection of the Treaty of Dardanus. Cynically Murena replied that he could find no proof of the existence of this treaty, which had never been ratified by the Senate. Of course it had not been ratified, for in 83 the Senate was controlled by the Populars, who had declared Sulla a public enemy and were at that moment fighting him in Italy. But the treaty had been formally promulgated by Sulla, Murena's commander; and in fact it was the only basis of his claim to be governor of Asia.

After plundering the neighbourhood of Comana Murena withdrew southward over the mountains to Cappadocia; he had not been opposed, and there had been no fighting. In the autumn Mithradates sent ambassadors to the Senate, to proclaim his peaceful intentions and seek protection from further forays by Murena.

Rome was still in the hands of the Populars, now led by Caius Marius, son of their old chief. (In practice democrats adhere to the hereditary principle more firmly than any oligarch.) But Sulla was slowly conquering Italy, and even a Popular Senate did not want a first-class foreign war on its hands. The Senators compromised by recognizing the irregular appointment of Murena, and then sending a commissioner to order him to keep the peace.

Before any message could arrive from Rome Murena moved again. Early in 82 he once more invaded Pontus. This second invasion came in from the south-west to cross the lower Halys. Again Mithradates held back his army, permitting the Romans to plunder without meeting resistance. He must have known that instructions from the Senate were on the way, and what those instructions contained.

In the valley of the Halys Murena plundered more than 400 villages, and then retired once more into Roman territory. Mithradates was in a situation of appalling difficulty. From the first war he had just managed to extricate himself with his hereditary dominions intact, and so far his born subjects were still loyal to him. But in the last resort despotic rule depends upon the personal authority of the ruler; if he could not protect his subjects they would seek a stronger guardian. Yet if he fought the Romans and was beaten for the second time his soldiers might desert such an unlucky leader. Archelaus, who could appreciate every factor in the situation, had shown by his change of sides that he saw no future for an independent Kingdom of Pontus.

Mithradates could only wait patiently, in the hope that the arrival of the Senate's commissioner would put an end to his troubles. Sure enough, when Calidus reached Murena's head-quarters he announced that the Senate considered itself bound by the Treaty of Dardanus. Mithradates had been reinstated as the client and ally of Rome, and Murena must not molest him.

That was satisfactory, as far as it went. But efficient secret agents kept Mithradates informed of all the private actions of his adversaries. He was told that after Calidus had delivered his public instructions he had been closeted in private with Murena; and this Calidus was another of those minor Roman politicians who saw Asia as nothing more than a fruitful field of plunder.

The Statesman

So long as civil war raged in Italy the Senate was powerless to punish or reward; Murena might disobey its orders with perfect safety. Calidus had intrigued to get his appointment, hoping to return to Italy a rich man; the wealth he looked for could come only from the ravaging of Pontus.

Therefore the King was not surprised when the Romans once more crossed his frontier. But now the last chance of peace was gone. After Chaeronea and Orchomenus a third defeat might be fatal; yet at any cost there must be a show of resistance. The army of Pontus might expect support from within the Roman province. The subjects of Murena and Ariobarzanes, oppressed by an undisciplined army and by a second generation of greedy Italian tax-farmers, would rise against their masters at the approach of a second army of liberation. Perhaps the glories of 88 would come again. As a beginning the veteran Gordius was despatched to Cappadocia, where he speedily gathered enough plunder to repay the sack of Comana. Mithradates himself led out the main army of Pontus to seek a decisive battle.

It is the misfortune of posterity that no contemporary man of letters was sufficiently interested in those lesser figures on the fringe of politics, Murena and Calidus, to write a tactical account of the campaign which followed. For it was a most interesting departure from all that had gone before. By midsummer in the year 82 Mithradates was on the verge of fifty, and he had been ruling for thirty years; yet never before had he commanded a great army. In his youth he had adhered to the oriental theory of kingship; and orientals regarded the rough business of fighting as beneath the dignity of a great King. He had been present at the siege of Rhodes very much as Louis XIV of France dropped in at the siege of some Flemish fortress; the operations were managed by subordinates, and he was there only to honour the Rhodians by receiving their surrender in person. At Miletopolis he had commanded troops; because an unexpected invasion called even the palace-guards into the front line. In both these encounters he had been beaten. Now, in middle age, he began his real apprenticeship to arms.

Perhaps this was because he could no longer trust hired experts. Archelaus had been treated very well. He had been given

93

a second chance after Chaeronea, though such a defeat was excuse enough for the dismissal of any commander; even after Orchomenus and his suspicious friendship with Sulla he was still welcome at the Pontic court. If the recipient of such favour could desert to the enemy, then no mercenary was to be trusted.

There may have been another reason. Mithradates had introduced a new tactical doctrine into his army, a linear formation which imitated the legion. Probably these thin lines, alien to the tradition of the close-packed spearmen of Asia, were unpopular with every veteran officer who had spent his youth learning how to train a phalanx. Any novel formation meets stolid passive resistance from the established military class, and unless the commander himself believes in it the new idea will be proved by demonstration to ensure defeat. Perhaps Mithradates knew that any mercenary general would put his new infantry back into the phalanx as soon as he had escaped from the eye of his employer.

We cannot reconstruct the details of the first campaign led by Mithradates in person, the crushing defeat of a veteran and confident army at the hands of a middle-aged novice. We can only say that a clash on the eastern bank of the Halys was followed by a Roman withdrawal over the river. A few days later Mithradates crossed in his turn, and found the Romans strongly entrenched on a hill. He stormed their camp, and drove them in rout into the pathless mountains of Phrygia. During the retreat Murena suffered further heavy casualties, presumably from the arrows of the Armenian bowmen.

At news of this great victory the whole of Cappadocia came over to Mithradates. But the cities of Ionia, remembering Sulla's heavy hand, dared not repeat the rising of 88; Mytilene alone declared for independence. The Roman siege of that strong city dragged on for many months, to give the young Julius Caesar his first taste of active service. But the Pontic army did not reach the Aegean, and in the end the isolated fortress must surrender.

Mithradates did not want another great war. Having shown to the Romans, and to his own subjects, that Pontus was still a formidable military power he sought an early peace. So did Sulla, who until November was engaged in conquering Rome. Early in 81 another Senatorial commissioner arrived in Asia.

Gabinius was not just a member of the Roman governing class, sent to mend his fortunes in the East; he was a man under authority, who spoke with the sword of Sulla to back his words. When he told Murena that he must abide by the terms of the Treaty of Dardanus he was instantly obeyed.

During the winter Mithradates had performed a religious rite of the highest significance. On the most sacred mountain in Cappadocia he offered the fire-sacrifice to the native war-god; in person he ignited the blaze, after carrying wood to the pyre on his own shoulders.

Appian hints at the importance of this rite when he says that it resembled the fire-sacrifice offered by the ancient Persian Kings at Pasargadae. Mithradates was informing his faithful subjects, the cavaliers and barons of inner Pontus, that he was done with foreign Greek customs, and would entrust himself and his Kingdom to the old gods of the land. The war-god honoured was not Ares, and in fact he had no counterpart in Greek theology. The Greeks could find no better name for him than Zeus Stratios, Zeus the Leader of Armies; but Olympian Zeus did not lead armies.

Henceforth Pontus would stand on her own feet, an outpost of the Persian culture which had once been the norm of civilization from India to the Hellespont; all western innovations were repudiated, whether they had been introduced by the Greeks who followed Alexander or by the modern and hated Romans. Seeing the pillar of fire on the holy mountain Pontic nobles of Persian blood knew what they fought for and loved what they knew.

The immediate objective was peace, and that was easily arranged at an interview between Murena and Mithradates. Once more the Treaty of Dardanus was promulgated, and the King promised to retire from all his conquests. In central Cappadocia these terms could not be carried out, for the nobles refused to recognize Ariobarzanes. A way was found round that difficulty. It was arranged that Ariobarzanes should marry an infant daughter of Mithradates, and that the disputed region should be the marriage settlement of the princess, administered by her father on her behalf until she same of age. The bride was only 4 years old, and thus could not be legitimate; since the Queen of Pontus had been nineteen years in her grave. But the daughter of an unimportant concubine was good enough for the unimportant King of Cappadocia.

Mithradates wound up the peace conference with a great banquet in the Persian mode. There were prizes for the heartiest eater, the deepest drinker, the funniest jokes and the best songs. Cappadocians of both factions, and some Romans, joined in the fun, though Gabinius held it beneath his dignity to take part. Here was another sign that Mithradates had put away the manners of Greece.

For more than five years there was peace. But Mithradates knew that one day, when the civil wars were finished, Rome would avenge 80,000 murdered Italians. Though he would not be the first to attack, he must build up his power against the day of reckoning.

The Roman aristocracy, the party at present in control of the City, did not wish to increase their dominions. So much was demonstrated in 81, the first year of the peace. When Alexander, King of Egypt, died in that year he bequeathed his realm to the Roman People. The bequest was not accepted, though neither was it formally refused. No Senatorial commission came out to settle the affairs of the Nile valley, where various unimportant Ptolemids continued to assassinate one another.

The official excuse given by the Senate, when eventually one was needed, was a high-minded doubt of the validity of King Alexander's will. The real reason, known to every statesman in the east, was that no commission of Roman Senators could get through the pirate fleets which now preyed on all shipping between Italy and the Levant. The pirates of Cilicia had come to control not only the Aegean but the western Mediterranean as well, right up to the Pillars of Hercules.

Though the death of Sulla in 78 put heart into the surviving Roman Populars the nobility continued to rule Italy and the City. Yet one group of provinces was still in arms for the cause of Marius and the Gracchi; in Spain Sertorius led an army of native Spaniards officered by Roman exiles and trained in Roman tactics. Other Populars, fleeing from Sulla's terror, had found a refuge in Pontus. All these refugees kept in touch with one another, and presently Mithradates himself sent envoys to the far west by the ships of his friends the pirates. Negotiations moved slowly and cautiously, for the Populars dared not come out into the open as allies of a notorious enemy of Rome; but by 75 a secret treaty had been concluded between Sertorius and the King of Pontus. Its terms are not known with certainty. The friends of Sertorius claimed that he refused to diminish the dominions of Rome, and promised to help Mithradates only in the defence of his hereditary frontiers; his enemies maintained that he had recognized the King as rightful ruler of all Asia. That was not really important to either party; a leader of guerrillas in Spain could neither cede Asia nor defend it. What mattered was that Sertorius sent to Pontus some of his military experts, including a certain Marcus Marius who may have been a son of the old demogogue. These were distinguished Romans who had held high office when the Populars were in power, veteran field officers who could train Pontic recruits in the tactics and discipline of Rome. From among the lesser exiles Mithradates made up a corps of 6,000 Roman foot, a full Roman legion.

During these years of peace all the troubles that beset Rome beyond the Adriatic were put down to the sinister influence of Mithradates. It was said that he had made a treaty with the barbarians of the Danube, and that the Thracians invaded Macedonia because he had bribed them. It is true that he was always in the market for stout mercenaries; perhaps some of them came from as far away as the upper Danube. But Thracians did not need a bribe to induce them to raid into civilization, and the illiterate savages who then lived in the modern Austria were incapable of concluding treaties with a King who ruled in another continent.

Behind every disorder the Romans saw Pontic intrigue, as some of us nowadays see Communist intrigue behind every strike. The actual events of the years 80–75 suggest that Mithradates wished for peace, if he could have it with security. His dealings with Sertorius and the other Popular rebels were a sensible reinsurance; but he did not intervene when in 77 the Romans were hard pressed in Macedonia, or in 78 when Servilius took measures against the Cilician pirates.

Instead he turned his attention to the Euxine. While his son Machares strengthened the Kingdom of Bosporus at the expense of the neighbouring Scythians, an expedition was sent to conquer a queer tribe which occupied the coast between Colchis and the Sea of Azov. These savages habitually sacrificed to their goddess every shipwrecked sailor cast on their shore; but since they happened to call themselves Achaeans puzzled Greek geographers speculated on the reasons that could have reduced descendants of the heroes who destroyed Ilium to such a low level of culture. Presently these Achaeans admitted themselves beaten, so that in theory the whole overland route between Colchis and Bosporus was in Pontic hands; but they were disobedient subjects, and in practice any army which traversed their country had to fight its way through.

So long as the Roman sphere of influence did not extend east of the Halys, with direct Roman rule ending at the border of Pergamum, Mithradates could live at peace with the West. His southern frontier was a different matter. There men of the same stock, aboriginal peasants subject to Persian nobles, spilled over from the Kingdom of Cappadocia into Cappadocian Pontus; most of these nobles preferred Mithradates to Ariobarzanes. This brought constant friction between the two Kings, and a perpetual coming and going of embassies to Rome. At length Mithradates lost patience. In 78 he called on his son-in-law, King Tigranes of Armenia, to settle the Cappadocian question once and for all.

Tigranes had recently taken to calling himself Great King, King of Kings; he considered the promotion justified by his conquests from the decaying Seleucid empire. But such grandeur called for a bigger capital than the little hill-town of Artaxata. He had just founded the new city of Tigranocerta on the northern edge of the Syrian plain, and was looking for citizens to inhabit it. No army opposed his invasion of Cappadocia, and the campaign developed into a slave-hunt on a great scale. Thirty thousand Cappadocians were led captive to Tigranocerta. After that there was no more trouble from Ariobarzanes, who lacked even subjects enough to provide a guard for his palace. Since the Armenians went home without trying to enlarge their boundaries the Romans took no action beyond a formal diplomatic protest.

In the autumn of 75 Mithradates was 57; after a reign of thirty-six years he may have begun to hope that he would end his days in peace. He had no quarrel with his neighbours, though he knew that Rome would never be his friend. If the Romans had rested content with their already great possessions there need have been no Third Mithradatic War. *frequent*

The death of King Nicomedes of Bithynia in the winter of 75 fundamentally altered the political situation. That miserable puppet, so often restored by Roman arms, despaired of the continued independence of his country. He bequeathed his realm to the Roman People, as nearly sixty years before King Attalus had bequeathed Pergamum.

At Rome there had been a change of policy. In general the aristocratic party disliked expansion and the democrats favoured it; the whole ancient world acknowledged the truism that democracies are more warlike than oligarchies. But the Roman nobility had a special reason to favour peace; since the provinces were governed by last year's City magistrates, for every new province a new magistrate would be needed. But with the annual election of eight praetors and two Consuls there were already enough posts for the annual crop of well-connected politicians; the governing class did not wish to make room for more office-holders. That was another reason, besides fear of the pirates, why the bequest of the King of Egypt had been refused in 81.

In 75 the oligarchy still formed the government; but ever since the death of Sulla its power had been dwindling; at each election the Populars grew stronger. Civil war had emptied the treasury, and the Roman People had their customary exaggerated idea of the fabulous wealth to be found in any eastern Kingdom. The Senate, eager to increase its favour with the electorate, accepted without hesitation the bequest of Bithynia. At the beginning of 74 both the ex-Consuls of the previous year came out to organize the new province.

By now the Euxine had become the private domain of Mithradates. His ships were permanently stationed at the entrance to the Bosphorus, and his friends the pirates made it difficult for any foreign war-fleet to approach the Hellespont. He had fought the poor and warlike Achaean savages chiefly to complete his control of all the harbours in his own sea. The prosperity of his scattered lands depended on unhindered intercourse between Panticapaeum and Sinope.

A Roman fleet (that is, of course, Greek ships in Roman pay)

based on Heraclea, the Bithynian port east of the Bosphorus, would turn the strongest barrier in his maritime defences. Roman armies stationed in Bithynia could march by the flat coastal plain to invade the richest part of his dominions, the prosperous Greek cities of Sinope and Amisus; his mountain barrier in Cappadocia and Phrygia would be turned as completely as his naval barrier at the Bosphorus. For years he had struggled to win that mountain barrier, even to murdering his own nephew at a peace conference and slaughtering the Galatian chieftains at his own table.

Mithradates determined to attack before the Romans were securely established in their new province. It was a desperate gamble, all or nothing; for if he failed he could not hope for another lenient peace. But anything was better than waiting behind an indefensible frontier until the Romans were ready to take vengeance for the massacre of 88.

There was nothing to be gained by delay, for in the winter of 75 the general situation was as unfavourable to Rome as it was likely to be in the foreseeable future. In Spain Sertorius was at the summit of success; the main Roman army, led by Pompeius the most eminent of the younger Roman generals, was fully occupied in fighting him. The Italian cities which Sulla had conquered were recovering their strength, and the confused political situation promised an early renewal of the civil war.

The corrupt and incompetent aristocratic government of Rome was not prepared for war with Pontus. The governor appointed to the new province of Bithynia, Marcus Aurelius Cotta, was a politician with very little military experience. The only genuine Roman troops at his disposal were the two veteran legions which had first come east with Flaccus twelve years before. By mutiny these men had driven two successive commanders to suicide; and though they had been toughened by long campaigning they were bored with foreign service and near the end of their term of enlistment. If they were faced with another long and bloody war they would probably mutiny for the third time. The Greek cities of Asia were at the end of their tether, ruined by the exactions of Sulla and the Roman tax-farmers; in the war of 88 their walls had been battered and their young men killed, so that they were no longer very effective military allies. But the example of Mytilene in 79 showed that they would seize any chance to strike back at their greedy conquerors.

Mithradates spent the winter of 75 in gathering his army. No one noticed, for the attention of every Roman was concentrated on domestic politics and the revolt in Spain.

He collected 16,000 horse from his born subjects and the nomads of the steppe, all of much better quality than the hired cavalry the Romans could send against him. His foot numbered 140,000 fighting men, besides the servants and pioneers. Six thousand of them were Italian exiles, trained Roman legionaries; the others were organized in light flexible formations, and their commanders were Roman officers who had held high rank in their own army. It is said that he mobilized another hundred scythed chariots, the new weapon which had proved so ineffective in Greece twelve years ago; but not every ancient authority mentions them, and if he paraded them to raise the morale of his recruits it seems that he did not employ them on the battlefield.

At the beginning of the campaigning season of 74 Mithradates for a second time performed the fire-sacrifice to the native war-god, in the presence of his whole army. At a separate review of his fleet he encouraged his sailors by offering to Poseidon a chariot and four white horses. Of course he addressed his forces in the speech of justification which was a necessary formality at the opening of every campaign. What he said, as related by Appian, is a handy summary of the Pontic case against Rome.

He began by boasting of his ancestors. They were something to boast of, for his house had ruled in Pontus for nearly 200 years; and before Alexander marched east they had been Persian satraps of Achaemenid descent. The antique fire-sacrifice would have made the same point. He then claimed truthfully that during his long reign he had raised the petty Kingdom of Pontus into a power of the first rank. Turning to discuss his enemies, he remarked with little exaggeration that from sheer greed they had enslaved 'even Italy and their own fatherland'. After agreeing to the Treaty of Dardanus they had shown bad faith; their army was busy in Spain, and at any moment they might expect civil war; they had permitted the pirates, his allies, to gain complete command of the sea; they themselves had not a single faithful ally, nor a truly loyal subject; some of their noblest citizens had taken service in the Pontic army.

All this was true. When he added that he had beaten the Romans whenever he encountered them he must have relied on the short memories of new recruits. On the Halys he had won, but at Miletopolis the Fimbrians had beaten him. Still, even that was a colourable boast.

With hearty cheers the Pontic army set out, 156,000 strong, for the invasion of Bithynia.

IV

The General

The Third Mithradatic War began with the invasion of a Roman province by a foreign power; but it was also a move in the world-wide struggle between democracy and oligarchy. There were enough Roman exiles in the Pontic army to make up a full legion; Roman experts trained many other formations. Mithradates had concluded a treaty of alliance with Sertorius, far away in Spain; he expected to find other allies among the subjects of Rome, and especially among their oppressed Greek subjects in Asia.

But a war for democracy was not quite the same thing as a war for the liberation of Greek cities from the greedy power of Rome. Marius in his old age had moved very far to the left, and the exiles who kept up the struggle after the death of their leader were naturally the most extreme members of the faction. Mithradates was surrounded by advisers who considered themselves to be experts in Roman politics; advisers out of touch with home; advisers who, after the manner of all exiles, exaggerated the strength of their support among their own people. Advised by these fanatical Populars Mithradates campaigned as the champion of freedom. He announced that in the territories he should conquer all slaves would be free men and citizens, and that the lands of Ionia would be divided among their inhabitants.

A programme of manhood suffrage and nationalization of the land did not appeal to every Greek; such extreme views were too much even for some Roman Populars. At that time young Julius Caesar was in Asia, studying rhetoric in the famous school of Apollonius at Rhodes. He had been born into a family of leading Populars; his aunt had married the great Marius, who had nominated his 14-year-old nephew to an important priesthood. He was a young man on the threshold of a political career, known to be eager for military glory. Yet when the invasion came young Caesar put country before party. He joined the militia which was raised for the defence of Asia by the proconsul Caius Aurelius Cotta, a relative of his mother. The defection of young Caesar must have disappointed the fanatical extremists at Pontic headquarters.

For the same reason, fear of a complete social revolution, the Ionian cities did not rise against the Roman yoke. To landowners and merchants even Roman tax-gatherers seemed a lesser evil than a wholesale distribution of property. But in most of these great towns there was a strong revolutionary party, so that the Romans in Bithynia could not neglect their rear.

Of course the Galatians were foes to the Persian stranger who had murdered so many of their chieftains. They were more formidable than they had been fifteen years earlier; for that very massacre had cleared the way for the rise of a capable chief, a Gaul named Deiotarus, who died many years later as acknowledged King of all the Galatians. In 74 the army he raised among his own people not only defended his country but occupied most of Phrygia. Thus in the central uplands there was now for the first time a native army dependably loyal to the Roman cause.

But the Bithynians were enduring their first year of Roman rule. There the citizens welcomed any invader who promised freedom. The great invasion from Pontus carried all before it.

Without a battle Mithradates entered the Bithynian capital, Nicomedia, as Cotta the proconsul fell back in haste to Chalcedon. That was a strong fortress, with a good harbour on the Bosphorus. Other Roman officials fled there, bringing small detachments of troops; and the warships in Roman service which had been sent to take over the Bithynian naval arsenal at Heraclea retired from the Euxine to join them. Most important of all, the prosperous and nominally independent city of Cyzicus, on the Asiatic shore of the Propontis, adhered firmly to the Roman alliance. The Cyzicene citizen-levy, to the number of more than 3,000 hoplites, marched overland to Chalcedon. By the time Mithradates arrived before the fortress the unwarlike proconsul found himself at the head of a considerable force.

The General

Until help should arrive from Italy the Romans could not take the offensive. Cotta was strongly inclined to shut himself up in Chalcedon and defend its walls until relieved. His subordinates thought such a passive defence would be disgraceful to Roman arms; in particular Nudus, the Roman naval commander, was eager to fight a pitched battle as soon as possible. That was a thoroughly sound plan; for a Roman victory would halt the invasion, while a defeat would leave them no worse off, provided they were not driven from the town.

Cotta refused to come out and fight in person, but in the end he permitted Nudus to lead out the Roman army. This of course contained very few Roman soldiers; it was made up principally of the Greek citizens of Chalcedon and Cyzicus, and of Greek sailors from the fleet. Nudus took up a strong position in the plain outside the city; but the Pontic attack dislodged him. As his men retired they became entangled among the garden-walls of the suburbs. He was unable to break off the action and retreat as planned behind the strong walls of Chalcedon. As the battle neared the walls Cotta lost his head and commanded the gates to be closed. Nudus and some other senior officers escaped by climbing up ropes let down from the wall; but 3,000 soldiers were butchered under the eyes of the timid proconsul, and many more were taken prisoner.

We know that Mithradates commanded in this battle. Unfortunately our authorities say nothing of his exploits; they do not even tell us whether it was the Pontic horse or the infantry who broke the Roman line. Probably the victory should be credited to the Cappadocian horse, for Nudus can have had hardly any cavalry to oppose to them. We know also that Mithradates in person gave orders for the full exploitation of his success. In obedience to his commands the Pontic fleet attacked the harbour while fighting still raged outside the walls. The attackers broke through the bronze chain which barred the entrance, rowed right into the anchorage, sank six Roman ships and towed away the remainder, to the number of sixty. This was a daring feat of arms; for if the harbour was so narrow that its entrance could be closed by a chain the whole area must have been commanded by engines mounted on the city walls. In the capture of sixty ships and the destruction of six others the loss of the Pontic fleet was twenty men only.

The General

Thanks to this victory the Pontic navy gained complete command of the Bosphorus and the Propontis. Narratives studded with unidentified place-names tell us little about the events of the next few weeks; but it seems that Mithradates ignored the small land-force remaining in Chalcedon, and moved tentatively towards the Bithynian border of Phrygia, where there was news of another Roman army. Practically the whole of Bithynia had been added to his dominions. If he could clear this army out of the way the road would be open to the great cities of Ionia.

This second Roman army was a formidable force of five genuine Roman legions, led by a good general. Lucullus was already a veteran of eastern warfare, the able lieutenant who had conjured up a fleet out of nothing while Sulla besieged Piraeus. He was popular among the Greeks of Asia, where he had done his best to mitigate the harshness of Sulla's exactions. In Rome he was trusted by the Senate, as a faithful adherent of the nobility who was himself without dangerous personal ambition. He had been elected a Consul for the year 74 (his colleague was Marcus Aurelius Cotta, brother of the incompetent defender of Chalcedon). As Consul he should have stayed in Rome throughout his period of office; but he was on bad terms with Pompeius, commander of the army fighting Sertorius in Spain and the most powerful figure in Roman politics. Octavius, propraetor in Cilicia, had died suddenly in office, and Lucullus, after some rather discreditable intrigues among the boudoirs and bedrooms of the nobility, received permission to replace him immediately. Shortly after the outbreak of war he arrived in Cilicia with one newly-raised legion, and two others which he had picked up in Macedonia. When to these were added the two veteran but disorderly Fimbrian legions he commanded a force of 30,000 Roman foot. But he was weak in cavalry, like most Roman commanders; he had only 2,500 mercenary Galatian horse to oppose the 16,000 Persian cavaliers who followed the King.

The advent of Lucullus, that known friend of Greeks and honest governor, decided many of the Ionian cities to remain loyal to Rome. He had leisure to make his plans, for another force lay between Mithradates and the legions. At this period the unswerving loyalty of Deiotarus was of the greatest value to the Roman cause; his fierce Galatians formed a screen on the Phrygian border, and the Pontic scouts could not observe the movements of the Romans in Cilicia.

Mithradates was undecided on his next move; like every other undecided commander, he squandered valuable time. Many cities on the Asiatic shore of the Propontis had declared for him, in particular the important harbour-town of Lampsacus. The citizens of Chalcedon were thoroughly frightened, and would probably ask for terms after his next victory. But Cyzicus remained as a focus of pro-Roman sentiment, and the irregular levies of Deiotarus lay too near for comfort to the border of Pontus.

At the age of 58 Mithradates was leading his first important campaign. In these puzzling circumstances it was natural that he should hesitate. He sent a squadron of pirate ships to dodge their way to the other end of the Mediterranean and get in touch with Sertorius; he sent a detachment of his army to watch Deiotarus, and another to blockade Cyzicus. With his main force he advanced gingerly in the direction of Cilicia, not especially eager for battle but anxious to learn what Lucullus was doing.

Archelaus, the old mercenary who had been defeated at Orchomenus, had been living quietly on his rich estate in Euboea, well behind the Roman lines. That estate tied him to the Roman cause; but he could not keep away from such a fascinating war. He turned up uninvited at the headquarters of Lucullus. There he pointed out a self-evident fact which must have been troubling the sleep of Mithradates; the Pontic army lay to the north-west of the Romans in Cilicia, but Sinope and the heart of Pontus lay directly to the north. Lucullus might leave Deiotarus to occupy Mithradates, and himself invade the undefended homeland of the enemy.

Lucullus acknowledged the wisdom of this advice, but he did not follow it. He was having trouble with his men, especially with the turbulent Fimbrian legions; and though in these circumstances a Greek general would have looked for easy plunder the Roman antidote for military discontent was always a pitched battle. He advanced through Phrygia to the border of Bithynia.

At a little place named Otryae the two armies made contact.

The General

There followed a puzzling interval of indecision, until they parted without fighting. It seems that at the beginning Lucullus was eager for battle; while Mithradates, who outnumbered him by at least three to one, refused to be drawn from his fortified camp. Then Marius, the chief among the Popular exiles serving with the Pontic forces (he had been a Senator before his flight), insisted on drawing out the legion of Popular exiles, with other detachments commanded by Roman renegades. Lucullus prepared to attack him, and the battle was about to begin; when an object fell from the sky between the two armies, an object like a flaming cask, seeming to be made of molten silver. Amazed by this mysterious omen, both sides retired.

A large meteor may have fallen as related. We must remember that both armies had good reason to be nervous; throughout Asia the Romans were believed to be invincible, and the mercenaries of Mithradates would recall Chaeronea and Orchomenus. But the Romans also, very far from home, knew themselves to be greatly outnumbered; and though Lucullus was a good soldier there was as yet no reason to put him in the same class as Sulla. Perhaps on both sides frightened men snatched at an excuse to retire without dishonour.

But perhaps Appian, our main authority for this incident, never learned the whole story. On the initiative of Marius, the leading Popular exile, two bodies of Roman troops were drawn up to fight what was practically another round in the long-continuing civil war; then they parted without a sword drawn. It is possible, especially in the light of advice given by Marius in front of Cyzicus later in the campaign, that treachery had been planned and that someone's nerve failed him at the last minute. Perhaps Marius expected the Fimbrian legions to come over to the Popular cause; and when he saw them steadfast in their ranks was glad to withdraw at the first opportunity.

Whether for supernatural reasons or not, no battle was fought at Otryae. Mithradates led his men straight to the siege of Cyzicus; Lucullus followed slowly and cautiously, for the land had been ravaged and it was difficult to procure food.

The citizens of Cyzicus determined on a stout resistance, even after the King in person had sat down before their town with more than 100,000 fighting-men. Their walls were strong, and well-sited for defence. Cyzicus lay at the extremity of a peninsula; on three sides it was protected by the sea, and the harbour lay safe behind a narrow entrance. Attack could come only up the neck of the peninsula.

By forming the siege Mithradates voluntarily bottled up his own army. Lucullus had only to march into the base of the peninsula behind him, and he would lose his land communications with Pontus. But the risk was worth taking. The Pontic fleet enjoyed absolute command of the sea, so that communication by land was not essential; and Cyzicus was a hostile port of entry into the newly conquered realm of Bithynia. Its capture would remove all danger of a Roman landing, for otherwise from Heraclea to Lampsacus all the Bithynian coast was in Pontic hands. Besides, the danger of a Roman attack from the rear was more apparent than real; at the root of the peninsula the mountains of Adrasteia made an impregnable position, where a part of the besieging army could dig in to face the mainland. Speed was what mattered, a quick victory to impress waverers. Mithradates pressed the siege with all his energy.

Although at the age of 58 the King had had little experience of war, he had for many years carried out important public works; he was competent to direct massive projects of engineering. In a very short time he had hemmed in the landward side of Cyzicus with an impregnable trench, and built out into the sea a double mole which blocked the harbour. As soon as the investment was complete he began to batter the defences. Engines mounted on high artificial mounds cast stones at the wall, and rams sheltered by penthouses were driven against it; in particular one great siege-tower was built to a height of 100 cubits. Outside the harbour a *sambuca* was constructed, even greater than that which had failed at Rhodes fourteen years before. It rested on two quinqueremes, and was equipped with a wide drawbridge.

The summer was consumed in these siege-operations. In other parts of Asia the war was going well. Pontic forces under a mercenary general named Eumachus conquered Phrygia and penetrated into Cilicia, killing many scattered Italian settlers with their women and children. Eumachus had to retire when Deiotarus of Galatia marched against him, but in general he held his own; and once Cyzicus had been taken Galatia would lie open to invasion.

Then Lucullus arrived, at the head of his five legions. Mithradates was unwilling to fight a decisive battle with Cyzicus untaken in his rear; but there was no need to do anything of the kind. Part of the army could hold off the Romans, while the remainder pressed the siege of the city.

But the Roman refugees in the Pontic camp were free with their advice. Marius was certain that the Fimbrian legions would never fight against eminent Populars such as himself; every demagogue is quite certain that he enjoys the esteem of his fellow-citizens, for otherwise he would not have the heart to continue at his degrading occupation. But the demagogue is nearly always mistaken. Marius insisted that he had only to show himself to the Fimbrians, and as soon as they heard his voice they would come over to the King. But he added that after swords had been drawn it would be much more difficult for them to change sides; once they had fought their way into the peninsula they might continue to fight for their oligarchic commander.

Mithradates was persuaded by this fatal advice. Probably it was given in good faith, but by following it he threw away his last great army. Never again, though he fought for the rest of his life, did he command a force which outnumbered his enemies; never again did he have a reasonable chance of expelling the Romans from Asia. Afterwards he fought because he had no hope of quarter if he surrendered, not because he expected to reign in Ionia as Great King. Now he ordered his troops to evacuate the impregnable position of Adrasteia, and permit the Romans to approach unhindered.

Of course the Fimbrians did not change sides. When they left Rome they may have been partisans of democracy; but that was many years ago, and now they were veteran professional soldiers. Exiles can never understand that they are forgotten by their countryman as soon as they have run away. Thus Mithradates was truly cornered, between Lucullus on Adrasteia and the strong walls of Cyzicus.

Unless Cyzicus fell quickly there would be no way out. But the Pontic engineers must have thought it still too early for an assault, for to begin with the King tried moral pressure. Three thousand Cyzicene prisoners were paraded on shipboard before the harbour defences; presumably these were the men captured in Cotta's defeat outside the closed gates of Chalcedon. They were brought close enough to speak to the garrison on the wall, and there appealed for immediate surrender as their only chance of mercy.

Such an appeal carried great weight with any Greek community. Even the Spartans, who usually preferred death to dishonour, had made an unfavourable peace with Athens to save the prisoners captured at Sphacteria; and though that was 300 years in the past the famous event was remembered by every educated Greek. But the men of Cyzicus stood firm. From the wall their leader, who bore the famous name of Pisistratus, answered that soldiers who had surrendered must not attempt to influence the actions of those who still fought.

These Cyzicene prisoners are not mentioned again. Presumably they were killed then and there. But many Greeks and Romans, like the modern Japanese, held that a man who laid down his arms when he might have died fighting had forfeited all claim to consideration.

Of course the citizens were looking anxiously for the Roman army of relief, known to be somewhere in the neighbourhood. The camp of Lucullus on Adrasteia was actually in plain view from their walls. But Mithradates feared that the defenders would resist stubbornly if they knew help was so near. The Pontic outposts were instructed to shout that King Tigranes had sent a great army to the help of his father-in-law; there lay the Armenian camp, in rear of the Pontic huts. The Cyzicenes were greatly discouraged, but they still defended their walls.

This state of affairs was too precarious to endure. Immediately after the appeal of the prisoners had been rejected Mithradates ordered a general assault, though it is clear that the preparatory battering was not sufficiently advanced. Without warning, in the middle of the day, the great *sambuca* was towed forward. For once the clumsy contraption behaved as its makers had planned. The ships reached the sea-wall, the bridge was lowered, and the column of assault dashed forward.

Mithradates should have been with them himself, waving a sword in the front rank. But he had been brought up to think that it was part of the greatness of a King that he waged war by remote control, and he had not yet unlearned the faulty lessons of his youth. It seems that there was not even a senior officer on the flying bridge; ordinary infantry led the assault, and they were not quite so determined as they might have been. The four bravest men in the detachment had naturally worked their way to the front rank; when they had run across the high, swaying bridge their comrades hesitated to follow them.

As the great *sambuca* bore down on them the citizens wavered. Just in time they rallied, killed the handful of isolated heroes, and poured blazing tar on the two quinqueremes until they withdrew out of range.

The assault on the landward wall started late, though it should have been synchronized with the advance of the *sambuca*; the defenders had just time enough to rush their reserves from the harbour to meet it. Desperate fighting continued until nightfall. The Cyzicenes dropped coping-stones on the battering-rams, or caught them in nooses; cushions of wool, or loose screens of linen, broke the force of stones cast from the catapults. Only in one part of the wall did the blazing barrels of tar thrown by the engines take effect; mortar powdered under the intense heat, until the stones collapsed in a random pile. But the stones themselves glowed red-hot, and the attackers flinched from scrambling over them; by the time they had cooled the citizens had piled another wall in rear of the breach.

As the day wore on the wind increased. By evening a full gale was blowing, and as the assaulting columns retired many of the most valuable Pontic siege-engines were left exposed in the front line. Since both sides were casting barrels of blazing tar in all directions the inevitable happened. As the gale rose the machines burned fiercely. By next morning Mithradates was back at the beginning again, with a disheartened army and no siege-engines.

His army was worse than disheartened, it was beginning to be hungry. When Lucullus occupied Adrasteia his men expected to fight at once, and they were a little reluctant to encounter such superior numbers. Lucullus was not in general very happy in his handling of troops, but at this time he was for once sensitive to the state of their feelings; he announced that there would be no battle, but that instead he would starve out his foe. During his advance he had picked up a few prisoners; by questioning them he discovered that on the barren peninsula Mithradates was feeding a total of 300,000 mouths. That in itself was evidence of weak administration. The Pontic army

contained at the most 100,000 fighting-men; the invading
soldiers had been permitted to pick up in the countryside as
many women and servants as they chose. In an army so laxly
governed it would be difficult to enforce a regular distribution
of short rations.

All fell out as Lucullus had foreseen. During the calm
weather of autumn the huge assembly in the Pontic camp was
supplied from the fleet. But so long as the Cyzicenes defended
their harbour the besiegers must land their cargoes on open
beaches, and with so many mouths to be fed it was impossible
to build up a reserve. When the first storms of winter interrupted the daily unloading the undisciplined army passed in a
single day from plenty to starvation.

There had been no time of shortage to give warning to Mithradates, and he did not recognize immediately the gravity of
his plight; just as, in roughly similar circumstances, Napoleon
retreating from Moscow did not recognize at once that *all* his
draught-horses would be dead in a few days. Mithradates was
not even a veteran commander; he was conducting his first
campaign.

Cyzicus also was hungry, and there were rumours of a capitu-
lation. If he could only hang on until he had won the good
harbour at the tip of the peninsula Mithradates would have
outwitted Lucullus. He decided to stick it out for as long as he
could. Winter had begun, and the Cyzicenes would not look for
relief before next spring at the earliest. If they accepted the
lenient terms he offered all could be regained.

It was Archelaus who destroyed the last chance of a Pontic
victory. Lucullus was an able general and an honest and
humane governor. But he carried to excess the typically Roman
disregard of 'public relations' and 'psychological warfare'; as is
shown by his troubles in after years with legions still discontented after he had led them from victory to victory. He had
brought his army to the right place at the right time, and the
war was going well. He assumed that his allies would do their
duty, as he did his duty. If he could inform the Cyzicenes of his
presence that would be an advantage. But the Pontic army
barred the way, and the Pontic fleet commanded the sea; so
for the present he could not let them know.

Archelaus, a Greek who understood the minds of Greek

H   113

The General

soldiers, saw the desperate importance of getting in touch with the besieged city. He sent messenger after messenger, until at last one got through. The hungry and frightened Cyzicenes learned that the great host entrenched on Adrasteia was the expected army of relief, not Armenian reinforcements for their foes. They determined to hold out a little longer.

Then they were encouraged by a striking manifestation of the favour of heaven. The city of Cyzicus was especially dedicated to Persephone, who was said to have passed that way on her journey from the Underworld. The greatest event in its religious calendar was the winter sacrifice of a fat heifer to the guardian goddess. During this winter of siege there was not a heifer left in the town, and the citizens reluctantly decided to offer as a substitute a model made of dough. But on the morning of the annual festival a fat heifer was found swimming in the harbour; she had strayed from the herd sacred to the goddess which was pastured on the mainland behind the lines of the besiegers. She walked of her own accord to the altar which awaited her. There were other stories of divine intervention. The town clerk announced that Persephone had appeared to him in a dream; and it was said that at Ilium Athene had been seen, her panoply scarred by the blows she had warded from her faithful people of Cyzicus. So long as the gods fought for them there could be no thought of surrender. In these rumours, and in the timely appearance of the dedicated heifer, we may perhaps recognize the agency of that expert in propaganda, Archelaus.

Mithradates did not venture a second assault, but continued his efforts to sap a way into the city. A great mound was built against the wall, and mines driven under it. But now there was sickness in his camp, besides such a lack of food that stories of cannibalism were current. Worst of all, the horses of his cavalry, the one arm in which he surpassed the Romans, were dying for lack of fodder. Though he clung to his purpose it was essential to preserve the cavalry, who could in any case play little part in a siege. When he heard that Lucullus had moved out with the bulk of his forces to clear away a Pontic outpost which menaced the Roman communications, Mithradates seized the opportunity to send off his cavalry to the plenty of Bithynia.

The King was learning the military art, which he had begun

114

to practise so late in life. He could snatch a fleeting chance, and make up his mind quickly. But he was not yet a sound judge of the morale of his own troops; and because Lucullus had been sitting still for so long he had forgotten how quickly Romans could move if they wanted to.

Snow was falling, and the hungry troopers were more anxious to preserve their horses than to make good speed. Lucullus spotted the movement as soon as it was made, and at once launched his foot in an all-out pursuit through deep snow. Many legionaries collapsed exhausted by the way, but the remainder caught up with the Pontic horse while they were gingerly preparing to cross the swollen river Rhyndacus. By an astonishing feat of arms the tired infantry charged and broke firm squadrons of cavalry. The Romans captured 15,000 men and 6,000 horses, and killed thousands of camp-followers.

About this time news reached Pontic headquarters that Deiotarus and his Galatians had defeated Eumachus and were reoccupying Phrygia and Pisidia. In despair, the King decided to abandon the siege of Cyzicus.

That he got away at all is evidence of military skill, though his army lost heavily in the retreat; perhaps the military skill was not that of Mithradates, but of the Roman exiles at his headquarters. It was now early in (73,) the depths of winter when the open sea was barred to normal shipping. But the Cilician pirates who served the King were more than normal sailors. They put into the open beaches of the peninsula to pick up Mithradates, his staff, and his war-chest; and ferried them safely to Parius on the Propontis. The army, led by Marius, dodged round the lines of Adrasteia under cover of darkness, and set off westward for the friendly port of Lampsacus. Pursuing, Lucullus caught them at the crossing of a river, probably the Granicus. Marius lost 20,000 soldiers killed, and many prisoners. The victorious Romans massacred a vast number of camp-followers, so that it was said that 300,000 men, women, and children lost their lives in this encounter.

Lucullus made a formal entry into Cyzicus. The grateful citizens instituted 'Lucullian Games' in his honour, which were celebrated annually for many years after. Lucullus himself then set off on a tour of Ionia, to collect a navy; while his army marched to invest Lampsacus.

The General

Mithradates was sometimes too complacent when things were going well for him, but adversity brought out all the courage and energy in his character. It was still midwinter, but his pirate allies controlled the Propontis. He sent ships to carry the remnant of his army from Lampsacus to Nicomedia, and himself sailed thither from Parius. He lost many men by shipwreck, as always happened when the ancients tried the desperate expedient of a winter voyage. But soon he had assembled in Nicomedia a strong and reorganized army; while Marius, his best commander, clung on in Lampsacus with a picked garrison of 10,000 men.

All turned on the control of the sea. So long as Mithradates held Nicomedia Pontus was shielded from invasion. Lucullus could be delayed by the strong fortresses of Bithynia while the Pontic fleet sallied out from the Propontis to cut his line of communications in the Aegean. There was still hope of winning over the Fimbrian legions, though even Marius now recognized that an appeal to their Popular sentiments would not in itself be enough. The Pontic admiral Aristonicus was despatched with a large sum in gold, to see what bribery could do to reinforce the partisan prejudice with which they had left Rome fifteen years before. Marius ventured westward from Lampsacus, sailing through the Hellespont to attack Lemnos. If all went well Lucullus might be isolated on the borders of Pergamum and Bithynia.

But Lucullus, more than any other Roman, understood the importance of sea-power, and when serving under Sulla he had learned the business of enlisting a fleet. The Greek warships he collected in Ionia were placed under the command of a Roman soldier named Triarius. Triarius captured Apamea and sacked it, while a detached squadron occupied Prusias and pushed on inland to seize Nicaea, evacuated by its frightened Pontic garrison. Aristonicus was betrayed by his own men, so that he and his treasure fell into the hands of the Romans. This last disaster was a symptom of something even more dangerous; it proved that far-sighted traitors no longer feared the vengeance of Mithradates.

Meanwhile Lucullus himself ventured out to fight in deep water, as few other Roman commanders would have done. His superior fleet caught Marius with only thirteen ships anchored off a barren islet near Lemnos. Marius defended the island stubbornly, for as a renegade he could not hope for quarter. After stiff fighting he and a few survivors of his squadron were captured, and his exalted Senatorial rank did not save him from ignominious execution.

Without having fought any great battle Lucullus suddenly found himself master of the Propontis as well as the Aegean. His communications with Rome were secure, and, even more important, he could turn the line of Bithynian fortresses by venturing into the Euxine. Unless Mithradates fell back he would be cut off from his own Kingdom. The King saw this clearly, and prepared to evacuate Nicomedia.

He decided to retreat by sea, it is hard to see why; for there were excellent roads between Pontus and Bithynia. Probably he thought his rich war-chest would be safer on shipboard than in the midst of an unruly army; perhaps he feared to be caught at some river-crossing, as his men had been caught at the Rhyndacus and the Granicus; perhaps he preferred the sea because the pirates of Cilicia were better sailors than any the Romans could bring against him, while on land he had no troops who could oppose the legions. Whatever his reason, it was an unlucky decision.

The pirates, of course, pillaged the towns of the Propontis before they withdrew; they plundered among other places the little town of Priapus, and carried off from its temple the venerable and ancient wooden image of Artemis which embodied the luck of the place. The storm which struck them as they emerged from the Bosphorus was therefore attributed to the vengeance of the outraged goddess.

Sixty ships were wrecked, and 10,000 men drowned. The King himself was for a time in great peril. The great transport which carried him and the bulky furniture of his court drifted waterlogged and unmanageable. To the surprise of his officers he transferred to the most seaworthy ship in his squadron, though it was manned by pirates. That seemed an invitation to these masterless and faithless men to earn a free pardon by selling him to the Romans. But Mithradates made a practice of trusting ruffians, though he was cruelly suspicious of respectable Greek citizens, and more often than not his trust was justified. There was evidently about him a personal magnetism which appealed especially to scoundrels. The pirates conveyed him safely to Heraclea, the last town in Bithynia; and from thence he continued by sea to Sinope, his capital.

The campaigning season of 73 was nearly past. Mithradates had lost his army and his fleet and all his conquests; but his own Kingdom was still untouched, and he still had plenty of money. He guessed, rightly, that Lucullus would not begin an invasion so late in the year. During the respite of the winter he set about raising another army.

He wrote to his son-in-law, Tigranes of Armenia; though he must have known that the Armenians who had not helped him when he was chasing a Roman proconsul into Chalcedon were not likely to come to his aid after Lucullus had driven him from Bithynia. He wrote to his son Machares, viceroy in Bosporus, telling him to enlist more Scythian mercenaries. In the steppe there were always more Scythian volunteers than the wealthiest King could take into pay, and the only limit to their number was the amount of money available. Mithradates also sent across the Euxine an agent named Diocles, with money and presents for the Scythian chiefs.

But any sensible man could see that Mithradates was losing the war, and statesmen experienced in Hellenistic power-politics were quick to desert a sinking cause. Neither Tigranes nor Machares answered his letters; Diocles went over to the Romans, taking his great treasure with him.

Mithradates must fight the coming campaign with the resources only of his hereditary Kingdom of Pontus. There was a single gleam of hope in the threatening sky. Lucullus also had suffered heavy casualties, though rather from sickness and forced marches than in battle; and Lucullus could expect no reinforcements from Italy. The news from the west was all of a great revolt of slaves in Campania and Lucania. Spartacus the brigand led 70,000 trained gladiators and revolted prisoners of war, whose march threatened the city of Rome herself; and the main Roman army was still occupied with Sertorius.

During 72 the war moved slowly. Mithradates, now in his sixtieth year and his own prime minister and commander-in-chief, considered that time was on his side. Sertorius was as strong as he had ever been and, though the revolt of Spartacus was a nuisance rather than a danger, the Roman Senate for the time being would be preoccupied with home defence. Lucullus and his five legions were the only foes Pontus need face for some years to come; let them lose more men in exhausting sieges and long marches, while he trained another army of his faithful subjects.

The King therefore left his capital, Sinope, that cosmopolitan city on the exposed sea-coast. He moved inland to the district of Cabira on the river Lycus; here, in fertile country which his ancestors had ruled for countless generations, he gathered from among his own born subjects a small army of 40,000 foot and 4,000 horse. These numbers did not compare with the vast multitudes who had invaded Europe sixteen years before; but every man was absolutely faithful, they were fighting to defend their own homes and property, and the cavalry were the superb horsemen of the Persian governing class. Throughout the summer Mithradates trained his recruits, without exposing them to the hazards of a general action.

He was able to do this because Lucullus was also playing for time. For subtle and devious reasons the Roman commander thought that a long war might bring him victory without the risk of battle. Lucullus was in fact a general of the first class, but he fancied himself much more as a politician and diplomatist. He liked Greeks, himself lived as a Greek, and was popular with the Greek subjects of Rome. He had conceived the bright idea of winning over the Greek subjects of Pontus by peaceful negotiation. Rome was already firmly established in Galatia and Cappadocia; when the cities on the coast of the Euxine had admitted Roman garrisons Mithradates would be encircled, unable to leave the barbarous and unimportant interior where he still had a following. If need be, he could then be crushed in battle; but it was more likely that when his soldiers found themselves cut off from civilization they would desert him.

Before Lucullus could win over the Greek cities of Pontus he must first approach them. In the spring of 72 he concentrated his army in Galatia. His rear was completely secure; for Bithynia, Pergamum, Ionia, and all the lands to the west and south were now firmly in Roman hands. But Eumachus and Deiotarus had been fighting all over the Galatian-Pontic border; as a result the region was so wasted that no army could cross it. Deiotarus however rounded up 30,000 coolies; Lucullus made each man carry a sack of flour, and with this improvised transport marched his army through the man-made desert without risk of starvation.

His legionaries were beginning to be spoiled by the luxury of the east. They were willing to fight, and in fact eager for battle; but they had got into the habit of living by daily plunder. They were most reluctant to traverse the barren fields of the Galatian border, and threatened mutiny. Once they had reached the interior of Pontus, which had enjoyed good government throughout the forty years of the reign of Mithradates, they found such plenty that even the acquisitive habits of professional soldiers could not gather all the wealth that lay about them for the taking. An ox could be bought for a drachma, one day's pay; and a slave for four drachmae, which reminds us of what invasion meant to harmless civilians in the first century. This was perhaps the only time during these long wars when Lucullus was popular with the men under his command; but the intensive slave-raiding must have made him disliked by the local Greeks, whose goodwill he valued more highly.

The Roman fleet had coasted eastward from the Bosphorus. Murena, son of the old Murena who had behaved so badly in the Second Mithradatic War, commanded a column of Roman troops who laid siege to Heraclea, Amisus, and Sinope. While these towns still resisted, Lucullus pushed forward into the interior of Pontus, where he besieged a fortress named Themiscyra on the river Thermodon.

This fortress (it was not a town but a castle) was in Roman eyes not very far from fairyland. The valley of the Thermodon was said to have been the original home of the Amazons; the castle of Themiscyra was named after one of their long-dead Queens. If the legend of the Amazons had any foundation in fact (and it was widely believed throughout the Mediterranean world) it may have arisen when a nomad clan of beardless Mongols penetrated the barrier of the Caucasus to settle in this secluded valley. In America similar causes produced a similar result, and Spanish explorers who encountered beardless archers on the banks of a great river called that river the Amazon. But the varieties of human society are infinite; perhaps genuine Amazons in truth dwelt for a few generations in the valley of the Thermodon, finding fathers for their children among the strangers beyond the mountains.

In any case the siege of Themiscyra was an odd affair, appropriate to that strange countryside. The Romans began in the usual way, by building mounds for their siege-towers. Perhaps the castle stood on a steep hill which their mounds could not overtop, for presently they turned their energies to mining. Mining was a well-known method of siegecraft, even in the days before explosives. The attackers drove a tunnel under the wall, propping it carefully with stout timbers; when the tunnel was complete the chamber at the far end was filled with straw and oil, and then set on fire. If all went according to plan the supporting timbers were consumed by the fire, and as the tunnel caved in the wall above it collapsed also.

The defenders of Themiscyra countermined, according to the standard practice of the day. Their object was to break into the incomplete tunnel, drive out the miners, and burn the supporting timbers before the mine had been carried right under their wall. There followed the usual desperate little fights underground, as small bodies of men clashed by torchlight in the cramped tunnels. But the Pontic garrison disposed of other, less usual, weapons. They sent into the Roman tunnels not only soldiers, but bears and leopards and swarms of bees. Such creatures must have been awkward companions within a besieged fortress; but since the commandant could not hunt in the forest while the Romans were at his gate he must have laid in a stock of them before the siege began.

It is exasperating that we do not know the outcome of this remarkable defence. But our authorities are interested only in the deeds of Lucullus and Mithradates, and leave a great many minor questions in the air. It seems that Lucullus himself did not capture the place, for he moved back to the coast while it still resisted. Presumably the ingenious commandant stood out for favourable terms, and may even have continued to rule the castle as a subject of Rome. If Themiscyra had continued to be held for Mithradates after the rest of Pontus had been conquered, surely we should have heard more of it.

Unrest among his troops compelled Lucullus to return to the coast. He was never popular with his men, perhaps because he was more careful to protect civilians than to reward his army. Now his soldiers complained that they were stuck up here in the backwoods, besieging a petty castle, while down by the coast the wealthy towns of Sinope and Amisus might at any moment be plundered by their comrades under Murena. Rather than risk a mutiny, Lucullus led them where they wished to go.

It is astonishing that such a successful commander should have been so constantly in trouble with unwilling troops. Lucullus was not a tyrant; on the contrary, he was long remembered in Asia for his honesty, his generosity, and his kindness to the weak. But at heart he was more Greek than Roman; and as an oligarch of the old school, one of Sulla's most faithful supporters, he must have been from the beginning out of sympathy with the Fimbrians.

During the rest of 72 campaigning was at a standstill. The Romans held the whole of the Pontic coastline, except for the few cities which still resisted their siege-engines; outside Pontus they were supreme in Asia. But Lucullus would not advance on Cabira, to finish the war at a blow. Some of his subordinates reproached him for this delay, and he explained to them his perfectly cogent reasons.

Besides the garrisons of Amisus and Sinope, which were frequently reinforced, Mithradates had gathered at Cabira a willing and well-trained army of rather less than 50,000 men, his hereditary subjects who served him with complete devotion. But that was a very much weaker force than the great hosts which had overrun Pergamum and Attica, and it seemed to be the utmost limit of his strength; for a whole summer of recruitment had not increased it. If the Romans advanced before the King was ready for them he would probably flee to Armenia. Then it would be impossible to catch him without beginning a great war against an unknown power with whom the Romans had had few previous dealings. But if they waited until next year the King would probably stand to meet them; after the patriots of Pontus had been crushed in one great battle the country would become a loyal province of Rome.

In the spring of 71 Amisus and Sinope, blockaded, still held out for their King. Mithradates was past his sixtieth birthday, and he was following a way of life that was strange to him.

The General

Gone were the Greek banquets, the offerings at Greek shrines, the dilettante aesthetic triflings which were proper to a Hellenistic prince. Gone too, and this must have seemed strangest of all to him, was the sea. No ship anywhere fought under his colours; he was ruler only of the upland forests and deep valleys of inner Pontus. As in the days of his adventurous youth, his bedchamber was a tent and his feasts were got by hunting.

But his small army was composed of excellent material; Roman mercenary horse could not face his cavalry. If the Romans ventured into the wooded mountains he could cut their communications, drive in their foragers, and starve them into retreat. His strong castles, which dominated every pass in the mountains, would hamper the movements of any invader. The King decided to await attack.

The Romans must leave detachments to continue the blockade of the coastal cities, and probably there was need for small garrisons in all the ravaged lands of Asia. Lucullus was outnumbered by the small Pontic army, though he considered his men a match for it. The historians of antiquity knew so well the damage done to any country by the mere presence of troops that they seldom bother to mention it; as we see both combatants employing ever smaller forces every year we must call to mind the unploughed fields and burnt-out villages which year by year reduced the food-supply of Asia.

Mithradates was still King of Pontus, and if he fought well he might keep his ancestral inheritance. The bulk of the native population were loyal to their King; but there were a few traitors, as in every oriental despotism. As in every oriental despotism the traitors were men in high places.

When Lucullus began his advance Mithradates had his first experience of this high-placed treason. A chain of beacons stretched to the edge of the coastal plain, manned by scouts who would give him early information of any Roman movement; these scouts were commanded by a cadet of the royal house known as Phoenix (either 'the son of the Phoenician concubine' or perhaps simply 'Purple-face'.) With an odd scruple of conscience Phoenix carefully lit the alarm-beacons before he brought all his scouts over to Lucullus. Henceforth the Romans had guides who knew the trackless mountains of the interior; they could march straight on the hidden valley of Cabira.

The General

But when Lucullus reached the broad valley where the Pontic army lay encamped the first engagement went against him. The mercenary horse of the Roman vanguard encountered the barons of Pontus defending the threshold of their native mountains, and the mercenaries broke and fled. Pomponius, commander of the Roman cavalry, was taken unwounded, and led before the King. Mithradates already knew that he could not win the war, and was eager for peace if he could get favourable terms. He offered Pomponius his life if he would be his advocate at Roman headquarters, and apparently proposed to confer on him the high official rank of 'King's Friend'. Pomponius deliberately misunderstood the offer. He replied: 'If you yield to the Romans I shall be your friend; if not, I shall continue to be your enemy.' At this the Pontic chieftains clamoured for his immediate execution; but the King, who admired courage and fidelity, ordered him to be well treated.

The defeat of his horse put Lucullus in an awkward position. He was far from his base, in the heart of the enemy's country; and with infantry alone he dared not march over level ground. Luckily there were plenty of mountains in the neighbourhood, and he at once entrenched a strong camp on top of a hill. For several days in succession the Pontic army offered battle in the plain below, but the Romans dared not descend to fight. It was most humiliating, and made some waverers with the Roman forces wonder whether they had really chosen the winning side.

One of these waverers was a Scythian captain of horse named Olcaba, a noble from one of the nomad tribes who lived by the Sea of Azov. On his own initiative he devised a plan which very nearly altered the history of the Levant. One day he arranged that his horse, saddled and bridled, should be grazing just outside the main gate of the camp. He then called at headquarters, announcing that he bore important news for the commander. If he had succeeded in stabbing Lucullus, which was what he planned to do, the Roman army on the Lycus would either have retreated in great disorder or, more probably, surrendered to Mithradates; and perhaps the Romans would never have conquered the interior of Asia.

But Olcaba, poor untutored Scythian, knew nothing of the all-important Italian siesta. He timed his call for early afternoon, and of course was told that the commander-in-chief could not be disturbed. He tried to force his way in. The servants of Lucullus barred his way so vehemently that he thought his murderous intent had been discovered. Suddenly he fled away, jumped on his waiting horse, and galloped to the Pontic camp.

There is no evidence that Mithradates had inspired this attempted murder, though of course the Romans laid the blame on him; any Scythian prince could think of such a deed without help from outside. But his narrow escape made Lucullus eager to bring the war to a climax; and it so happened that the next example of treachery favoured the Romans.

A Roman patrol stumbled on a cave in which a few men were living. These men were Greeks, who claimed to be professional hunters; but to hunt bears and wolves for their skins is not a characteristically Greek way of living, and the native hunters of inner Pontus would not gladly suffer foreign competition. These Greeks must in fact have been bandits on the run, fugitives from the King's justice. Of course they were willing to help the King's enemies; they offered to show the Romans a hidden path over the mountains.

So long as Pontic cavalry dominated the valley Lucullus was in danger of losing his line of supply, which stretched northward to the coast near besieged Sinope. He decided on a daring move. On a dark night he left his watch-fires burning; guided by the Greek brigands he led his men by mountain tracks southward, skirting the plain on which Mithradates lay encamped. Next morning he was securely entrenched on another hilltop, upstream of the Pontic army; behind him lay a tangle of hills in which his foot must be safe from the King's horsemen, and a narrow and difficult pass through which supplies could reach him from Cappadocia.

Mithradates had been outmanœuvred. He drew his own supplies from the hill country to the south, and there lay the homes and families of his best soldiers; they would be tempted to desert if the Romans began to ravage southern villages and castles. In addition there was the danger that Murena marching up from the coast might drive him into the arms of Lucullus. The Romans must be dislodged, even at the cost of a pitched battle on broken ground where the Pontic cavalry could not charge.

The General

But if Lucullus would not leave his palisade there could be no battle. When the King drew out his army the Romans declined the challenge. An accidental encounter demonstrated to both sides that it would be prudent to act with caution. A Pontic hunting-party, in pursuit of a deer, made contact with the Roman pickets; the Romans tried to surround them, and their friends came to the rescue. More Romans reinforced the pickets, until large numbers were engaged on both sides. The Romans were getting the better of it when Mithradates in person rode out from his camp to take command. Encouraged by the presence of their King his men rallied, and it was the turn of the Romans to retire. Mithradates pursued them as far as the slope below their camp; even after he had halted his men the legionaries continued to run, everyone thinking that the footsteps of his comrades were those of a ferocious Pontic mountaineer at his heels. They could not be stopped until Lucullus himself rode among them.

The legionaries who had fled were publicly disgraced, according to the custom of the Roman army; they were set to digging trenches in fatigue-dress, unarmed, while their better-behaved comrades looked on and jeered. Mithradates issued a triumphant order of the day, and sent messengers to his faithful blockaded cities on the coast to announce a great victory. But in fact the position was unaltered. Lucullus must be dislodged from his trenches overlooking the Pontic camp; and since his palisade was too strong to be taken by direct assault he could only be compelled to move by the threat of starvation.

One factor had been altered. This accidental encounter must have taken place about the time of Mithradates' sixty-first birthday, and for the first time in his life he had displayed outstanding courage in the open field. We know nothing about the first action in which he commanded, at Miletopolis, except that he was beaten. Since then his army had been victorious, notably over Nudus and Murena, while under his personal command; but his own exploits were not considered worth recording. Now, in what was for those times old age, he rode among his fleeing soldiers as gallantly as Sulla at Orchomenus, and by his personal example stayed the rout. Lord Acton's dictum has sunk so deep into the consciousness of every student of history that we are inclined to overlook this example of absolute power, enjoyed for forty years, giving courage to its holder instead of corrupting him.

The campaign, like so many of the campaigns of antiquity, developed into a starving-match. Lucullus lay between Mithradates and the hinterland from which he drew his supplies; but convoys bringing corn for the Romans must fight their way through the Pontic cavalry. More than once the horsemen inflicted heavy casualties on the escort of the Roman baggage train.

About this time Mithradates would have heard two discouraging items of news, if he was still in touch with the outside world. Spartacus had met the usual fate of a leader of revolted slaves; thousands of his followers hung on crosses beside the Appian Way. Sertorius had been murdered by a jealous subordinate; his Roman lieutenants were quarrelling over the succession, and most of his native Spanish warriors had gone home. By the next campaigning season the west would be at peace, and the Roman field-army would be free for employment in Asia.

Then the Pontic cavalry, grown too daring, met with a crushing disaster. On the approach of a valuable convoy Lucullus sent out ten whole cohorts as escort; and ten cohorts of Romans, the equivalent of a full legion, was a very formidable force. When the Pontic horse attacked them they took refuge in a narrow ravine where there was no room for cavalry charges. Rashly the cavalry pushed in after them, and the Romans counter-attacked. The horsemen, caught against the steep mountainside, are said to have been killed to the last man. The story must be exaggerated; for if cavalry run away from infantry most of them will escape. Probably the horsemen scattered to their homes. It is certain that only a handful returned to Mithradates.

When the few survivors straggled into camp the King was appalled. He knew that his foot were incapable of facing Roman legionaries, and that without cavalry he must retire from the open valley. His only chance was to get away into the mountains, where he might gather more horse. But for weeks he had been under very great strain, and in this crisis he lost his head.

At the age of 61, with little previous experience of supreme command, he had for many days been leading his troops in bloody skirmishes and constant bickering at the outposts. The palisaded camp of his foes overlooked his own camp, and from hour to hour he must be ready for a pitched battle. The need to be continually on the alert had frayed his nerves, and the nerves of his soldiers. Now, in a moment, the odds against him had lengthened fantastically. There was only one consolation. The survivors of his cavalry had fled faster than the Roman infantry could pursue; he knew of his defeat a few hours before Lucullus would learn of his victory. If he acted quickly he might disengage while the Romans still feared to approach his army.

Though it was already nightfall he summoned his chief lieutenants and issued orders for immediate retreat. His officers pointed out that in such a hurried move it would be hard to safeguard the baggage. That baggage was most important, since for more than a year the camp at Cabira had been the financial and civil capital of Pontus. The King's treasure, his records, his regalia and the savings of his courtiers, all were carried with the baggage of his last army. Mithradates saw the force of this objection. He gave orders that the baggage should be got on the move before news of the impending retreat was made public to the army in general.

In this he betrayed his lack of military experience. He should have known that the staff cannot plan a move without servants telling cooks, and cooks telling their friends in the ranks. In a few minutes the whole army knew for a fact that the high command was going to sneak away by night, leaving the fighting soldiers to be butchered by the Romans. That kind of rumour is readily believed in any army.

Every soldier decided that if his betters were running away he owed it to himself to get a good start in the race. As the gates were opened to allow the baggage-mules to leave they were rushed by a crowd of hysterical fugitives. Senior officers who called on the men to halt were cut down; and once the soldiers knew themselves guilty of mutiny they naturally went on to plunder the precious baggage.

In this tumult Dorylaus was killed, the old general who had served with Archelaus in Greece. He happened to be wearing the costly purple dress-uniform of a Pontic general of division; he was murdered by men who assumed that such a splendidly dressed figure must be worth robbing, though in fact he was

The General

poor and honest. Among others slain was Hermaeus the chief priest; which shows that the mutineers were in the grip of blind panic, for no veteran would consider an army chaplain to be worth robbing.

As he tried to stem the rout Mithradates himself was very nearly killed. Mutineers tumbled him off his horse, and stole it. The King was left alone and on foot, gesticulating after his army as it streamed out of the gate.

Lucullus, in his camp on the hill, was soon aware of the tumult in the valley below. Though it was still dark the Romans advanced to the attack. Thereupon even the bravest Pontic soldiers fled blindly; and because their camp was in the middle of an open plain they fled in all directions. There was no chance that they could be rallied into one body when they recovered their courage in the morning.

Seeing that there was nothing else to be done Mithradates joined in the flight, struggling on foot along a dark and crowded road. The old man could not have kept up with the rout for long; but when capture seemed inevitable a faithful eunuch, who had recognized his master, dismounted and gave him his own horse. Even when mounted the King had little chance of escape; Roman cavalry were riding through and through his broken army, and the road ahead was blocked by fleeing foot. In this overwhelming and unforeseen disaster Mithradates kept his wits about him. He saw in the press a baggage-mule, and remembered that it carried a sack of gold; this cannot have been known to the soldiers who ran beside him, or they would have stolen it. He rode alongside the mule, and just as the Roman troopers overtook him cut through its panniers to spill its treasure on the road. The Romans, who of course were really Galatian mercenaries, halted to pick up the gold. By dawn the King was clear away.

Lucullus could not press the pursuit, for his infantry insisted on waiting to plunder the Pontic camp by daylight. In the course of the day a few loyal Pontic barons recovered their courage and sought out their leader. But after he had collected a bodyguard of 2,000 horse Mithradates understood that no more was left of his army, which yesterday had mustered 40,000 strong. Few of his men had been killed by the Romans; they had just disappeared to their homes.

I
129

The General

Mithradates could no longer carry on the war. He might have lurked in the hills until his army had assembled again; but what was the use of an army which broke up in panic when ordered to retreat? He could not submit to the Romans, since the great massacre of 88 was still unavenged. There was nothing for it but flight.

Yet everything was not lost. Amisus and Sinope still resisted valiantly, and throughout the hill-country castles were held for the King of Pontus; these castles contained hoards of gold and silver, as well as hostages and prisoners of state. Mithradates possessed assets, which might persuade a powerful ally to support his cause.

Armenia was the obvious ally. King Tigranes, his son-in-law, was already a mighty conqueror who had assumed the vacant title of Great King, King of Kings. His dominions lay beyond the Roman sphere of influence, and Lucullus might be reluctant to extend the theatre of operations without special instructions from the Senate. The army of Tigranes was especially strong in archers and cavalry, the arms in which the Romans were weakest. In the past Tigranes had overrun Cappadocia whenever he had a mind to do so; he could as easily expel Lucullus from inland Pontus, though without a fleet it would be impossible to free the coastal cities. Although the geography of this campaign is doubtful, for many of the places mentioned cannot be marked on modern maps, it seems that Mithradates had retreated eastward from the scene of his disaster in the valley of the Lycus, and that the Romans were to the west of him.

The road to Armenia was open. With his bodyguard Mithradates rode east.

When he had crossed the frontier he was dismayed at his reception. He asked to be taken at once to King Tigranes, but instead his little band of loyalists was interned in an Armenian fortress. He himself was assigned as a residence a lesser royal palace near the Pontic frontier, and he was forbidden to leave it. Tigranes would not even answer his letters, though he sent instructions to the local governor to see that his father-in-law should lack for nothing. Armenia did not dare to give offence to Rome.

For the only time in his life Mithradates gave way to dispair.

The General

There seemed to be nothing he could do to hinder the Romans from conquering his Kingdom. At least he could deny Lucullus some valuable trophies. Ruthlessly, he gave orders for the destruction of everything of value in his castles which could not be forwarded to Armenia.

The commandants of the hill-castles were instructed to bury the royal treasure stored in their care, and then to make the best terms they could with the Roman invader. Some of them carried out the orders of their powerless ruler with exemplary fidelity, for right up to the end of his life Mithradates could lay his hands on large sums of ready money. Others yielded to temptation; they handed over to Lucullus their prisoners and confidential archives, while they kept the treasure for themselves. In particular Strabo the geographer notes that his grandfather brought over to the Romans the fifteen castles in his charge. He was a kinsman of the old Dorylaus who had fought for Mithradates Euergetes in Crete, and one of the most powerful figures at court; but the number of castles that obeyed him gives us an idea of the magnitude of these great fiefs of inner Pontus.

A few political prisoners were rescued by the Romans. Of these the most important was Nysa, a younger sister of the King. She was now an elderly virgin, long past childbearing; Mithradates had condemned her to lifelong seclusion because he himself did not wish to marry her and she must not marry any lesser man. She was grateful to Lucullus; but a life passed in the dull privacy of the harem had unfitted her for politics, and nothing more is known of her. Another important prisoner fell into Roman hands, though by a stroke of bad luck he did not reach Lucullus. Callistratus had been the King's private secretary, and it was hoped that he would reveal various secret and discreditable Pontic intrigues; but he carried 500 gold pieces concealed on his person, and when his captors discovered the money they cut his throat before dividing it.

Most of the royal family had been lodged in Pharnacia, the town farthest removed from the threat of invasion, the last Pontic outpost on the frontier of savage Caucasus. Though the nearest Romans were still distant the King despaired of ever reaching them again; and Lucullus could take the place as soon as he should march thither. Mithradates commissioned a trusted eunuch, one Bacchides, to make away with any inmate of his harem who was worthy of a place in a Roman Triumph.

The most eminent ladies at Pharnacia were the King's two sisters, Roxana and Statira; and two once-favoured concubines, Berenice of Chios and the famous Monime. There was also a crowd of other women, female relatives of these great ladies, lesser concubines and maidservants. When all these had been assembled before him Bacchides announced that they must die; they were permitted to kill themselves in any fashion they found convenient.

At last these unhappy ladies of the harem might do one final deed to redeem their anonymous lives from oblivion. Roxana cursed her brother, and the fate which had cheated her of marriage and brought her to this squalid death; then with firm self-control she drank the traditional Pontic poison and died bravely. Statira imitated a Queen of classical tragedy. She told the eunuch to thank her brother for his kindness in remembering his family when he was burdened with so many cares, and for giving her the opportunity to die free, before she was raped and enslaved by Roman soldiers; then she also drank the poison and died.

The Ionians felt none of the compulsion of royal blood. Berenice shared a cup of poison with her mother; for death was inevitable, and this was the least painful gate to it. The older woman drank greedily, and succumbed at once; but she did not leave enough for her daughter, who writhed in agony until Bacchides strangled her, moved apparently by compassion to put her out of her pain. This is the first and last mention of Berenice in our authorities; she may have been quite a young girl, recently chosen from among his many Chiot captives by the elderly but vigorous King.

For Monime there was the added bitterness that her troubles were entirely her own fault. She must have been past her first beauty, for it was seventeen years since Mithradates had singled her out from the crowd as he entered a conquered Ionian city. At that time he had offered a great deal of money as the hire of her favours. Had she accepted his terms she would have ranked as a mere courtesan, free to take her fortune and go as soon as her protector was tired of her. Pride had made her stand out for royal ornaments and the status of a concubine, and there was the root of all her misfortunes. A royal concubine must be reserved solely for the royal bed. When the affair was over she could not take the wages of sin and enjoy herself in the raffish Ionian half-world; she must live cloistered with the other unwanted concubines. Now she must die, to satisfy the touchy vanity of her master. It all followed from her acceptance of that useless diadem. She tore the linen band from her head, and attempted to strangle herself with the flimsy ornament. It broke, and she spat on the treacherous thing before she begged Bacchides to cut her throat. Monime was as well known for her intelligence as for her beauty; in her last moments she must have been fortified by the knowledge that she was enacting the kind of edifying moral fable that would catch the attention of every contemporary historian, and ensure that so long as the Greek language is read she will not be forgotten.

Appian maintains that this ruthless destruction of royal ladies alienated many influential Pontic castellans. But Appian was an Alexandrian Greek, who did not understand the oriental feeling that a man's first duty to his womenfolk is to keep them from handling by the vulgar, rather than to ensure their continued existence. As we shall see, Mithradates retained the affections of his native subjects until the end of his life. Plutarch says more briefly that Lucullus was disappointed, for he had hoped for an opportunity to display his mercy; and that sounds more plausible. The Roman commander was cheated of a big scene, in which he could have emulated the clemency shown by Alexander to the captured family of Darius.

Meanwhile the Roman army advanced as far as the border fortress of Talaura, where Mithradates had stored his heirlooms. When they learned that the King had fled to Armenia they turned back, leaving the castle untaken, to subdue the open country of Lesser Armenia. Lucullus had no warrant from the Senate to make war on King Tigranes, and he hoped that a distinguished embassy would be enough to secure the handing over of the powerless fugitive. In the meantime it was more important to clear up the last nests of resistance on the Pontic coast. The Roman army went into comfortable winter quarters outside the blockaded cities of Heraclea, Amisus, and Sinope.

During the whole of the next year, 70, old King Mithradates

remained in helpless exile in a remote hunting-lodge belonging to the King of Armenia. His son-in-law would not see him, would not even answer his letters; there was a chance that he might be handed over to the Romans as soon as their embassy arrived at the Armenian court. Some of his bodyguard remained faithful; but guarding a dethroned King who was at best under house-arrest, at worst a war-criminal awaiting trial, was no life for a soldier. Most of them drifted either back to their homes or into the Armenian army.

During this year the last foes of Rome in any part of the civilized world were overcome, never to revive. In Italy the slave-revolt was extinguished with torture and mass-executions; in Spain the murderer and successor of Sertorius, Perperna, surrendered to Pompeius. Nowhere did a band of Populars remain in arms, to continue the civil war which had begun in the year of the birth of Mithradates. The Roman field-army was free to act against a foreign enemy, but there was no foreign enemy to fight.

Lucullus took his time about crushing the last islands of Pontic resistance. Every Roman commander was reluctant to admit that the war he was engaged on was finally ended, and that he no longer needed an army; in addition Lucullus was genuinely a friend to Greeks, and anxious to ensure by kind treatment the loyalty of his country's new subjects. Heraclea surrendered on favourable terms; but then Heraclea was in theory a dependency of what had been the Kingdom of Bithynia, bequeathed to Rome all of ten years ago.

The truly Pontic towns, Amisus and Sinope, resisted desperately for as long as their walls could be held. Both cities had their own squadrons of warships, and by hard fighting kept their harbours open. When the men of Sinope could hold out no longer they destroyed their heavy battleships, which were unsuitable for deep-sea voyaging, set fire to their city, and sailed away in fast cruisers and merchantmen. Lucullus, who felt great reverence for any colony founded by Athens, the exemplar of civilization, did his best to extinguish the fire. But his soldiers, intent on plunder, allowed the flames to spread until most of the town was burned to the ground. Nevertheless, Lucullus proclaimed that Sinope should remain a free city. Soon the fugitive citizens were persuaded to return. So long as the Roman commander in Asia was honest and humane they lived in some prosperity.

Amisus, another Athenian foundation, had received only seventeen years ago a fresh wave of Athenian immigrants, fleeing from the tyranny of Aristion. Hereditary love of freedom inspired them to a stubborn defence, until the Romans by a surprise assault during the dinner hour made a lodgement on the wall. These citizens also fired their own city and fled to their ships. Again Lucullus gave orders that the town should be saved, again his men disobeyed him. Again in the end he persuaded the citizens to return, to make a fresh start under the firm peace and heavy taxes of Rome.

As soon as the Pontic seaports were conquered Machares of Bosporus sent envoys to Lucullus. This is the first mention of him during the Third Mithradatic War; presumably he had sent tribute and recruits to his father, but he had not himself crossed the Euxine to command troops in action. Perhaps he is not to be blamed for deserting his father when all seemed lost; at least he was acting in character, for no one was surprised at his treason. Lucullus gladly recognized him as lawful sovereign of Bosporus, and until retribution overtook him he reigned contentedly as a Roman client-King.

We know nothing of Colchis at this period, but it seems that the Colchians did not offer submission to Rome. Presumably while the war lasted they called no man master. But the rule of Pontus was remembered with regret, and later its return was welcomed.

These events should be remembered when we assess the merits of Mithradates as a ruler. In liberated Ionia he quickly wore out his welcome; the barons of inland Pontus followed him faithfully because he was head of the house which had ruled them from time immemorial. But the free citizens of Amisus and Sinope, men who inherited the traditions of Periclean Athens, fought for their barbarian King for as long as their walls were standing, and then were willing to endure exile rather than submit to his conqueror. For many years the reign of Mithradates was remembered as the golden age of these Athenian colonies on the Euxine.

When the last fortresses of Pontus had surrendered, Lucullus returned to the old Roman province of Asia, where he spent the autumn and winter repairing as much as he could of the economic damage inflicted by Sulla fourteen years earlier. The Ionian cities had paid the indemnity demanded by the Treaty of Dardanus; that money must be paid at once, or Roman soldiers would come to collect it with fire and sword. But they had paid only by borrowing from usurers, in general Italian usurers safe in the protection of Roman citizenship. Now their debts mounted, as unpaid interest was added to the principle. It seemed that soon every free Ionian must be sold into slavery to satisfy the perfectly legal claims of respectable Roman business men.

Lucullus put things right by enforcing the letter of the law, even against Romans and in favour of provincials; a course very seldom followed in Roman law courts. He reminded the money-lenders that the maximum legal rate of interest was 1 per cent per month, 12 per cent per year; and in his own discretion as proconsul he devised a bankruptcy law by which a creditor must take not more than a quarter of a debtor's income to pay the debt by instalments, instead of seizing his body and all his goods in default of full payment as soon as it fell due. A flicker of prosperity returned to Ionia, until in the next round of the Roman civil wars first Cassius and then Marcus Antonius plundered these unhappy cities to the last farthing.

Leaving behind him a peaceful and contented Asia, Lucullus was free to turn his attention to King Tigranes of Armenia.

V

The Exile

There was no necessity for the Romans to conquer Armenia, whose frontiers marched with the central Asian steppe where natural boundaries are lacking; an army composed of heavy infantry would find itself embroiled in limitless war when once it had penetrated to the unknown country beyond Lake Van. Since the dawn of history whichever Great King ruled in Mesopotamia (there was always a Great King, Babylonian, Assyrian, Persian, Greek, or Parthian) had left Armenia to enjoy self-government, provided the Armenian King kept within his own boundaries and offered a nominal tribute. The Senate in Rome was opposed to a forward policy, which would entail more provinces to be provided with ambitious and self-seeking governors and a dangerous increase in the strength of the army. The Popular faction, still out of office though its power increased daily, was traditionally the party of foreign conquest. But even the Populars did not want war against Armenia here and now; for they distrusted and disliked Lucullus, the faithful adherent of their great adversary Sulla. All parties in Rome hoped that the Pontic war would now be declared at an end, and that the dangerously successful proconsul would be compelled to come home before he grew too powerful for the constitution.

It is quite likely that even Lucullus did not want war against Armenia. His main interest at this time was to reconcile his friends the Ionian Greeks to the necessity of Roman rule, and he wished to stay near the Aegean where he could keep an eye on the Roman tax-gatherers. But precedent made it imperative that he should send an embassy to Tigranes, to demand the surrender of Mithradates; and his choice of an ambassador was circumscribed by family ties.

The Exile

Lucullus was at this time fairly happily married, for a Roman noble; though later his marriage, like most noble Roman marriages, ended in divorce. His wife had a brother, young Appius Claudius Pulcher, better remembered by posterity under the alternative spelling of Clodius which he adopted when he found his noble name a handicap in his chosen career of extreme left-wing politics. Young Claudius was able, intelligent and forceful, and his manners could be charming; before he died he proved himself a brave leader, whose men followed him with great devotion. But in the year 70 he was at the beginning of his evil and spectacular career, a mere military tribune who had seen little active service. Even his brother-in-law could not give him an independent command without provoking an outcry in the Senate. Yet there he was at general headquarters, aching to distinguish himself. With such noble birth, such great physical beauty, such overwhelming charm, he was the obvious man to send as Roman ambassador to King Tigranes of Armenia.

King Tigranes in his turn had no reason to go to war against Rome. He had ruled his native land for some twenty-five years, and had vastly increased his dominions. But he was a cautious and successful diplomatist rather than a dashing warrior. By about the year 83 he had made himself supreme in Syria, and had fixed his frontier with Parthia on the Tigris instead of the Euphrates; but he had done this by capturing one little city at a time, and by cunning intervention in the civil wars of the last Seleucids. To impress his subjects he encouraged pompous ceremonial, and had lately assumed the title of Great King, King of Kings.

In Rome it was taken for granted that Tigranes was the friend and ally of his father-in-law Mithradates; but during the more than twenty years of the marriage the alliance had been curiously intermittent. In 93 the Armenians had invaded Cappadocia to further the foreign policy of Pontus; but in the next year, when Sulla ordered them to withdraw, they went home without argument. In 78 they had ravaged Cappadocia for the second time. But anyone could ravage the realm of the miserable Ariobarzanes, and they had retired as soon as the Roman garrison in Cilicia seemed to threaten them. In 74, when Mithradates chased Cotta into Chalcedon and invested Cyzicus, the

Armenians stayed at home; though the opportunity for a combined attack on Roman Asia was so promising that the Cyzicenes assumed the second army to appear outside their walls must come from Armenia, not from Rome. Though Tigranes had given shelter to the fugitive Mithradates he had not received him at court.

If the Roman ambassador had been an experienced Hellenistic diplomatist of the kind Tigranes was accustomed to he would have begun by demanding the surrender of the King of Pontus, dead or alive. But he would have allowed it to be understood that what Rome wanted was peace in her new province, not the satisfaction of revenge on a powerless exile. So long as Mithradates hovered just across the border there would be danger of revolt. By all means let the Great King give shelter to his unfortunate father-in-law, but on the shores of the Caspian, for example; not within an hour's ride of the nearest Roman outposts.

Probably Tigranes would have seen the justice of this request; he had troubles of his own with insubordinate royal princes, as will appear hereafter. Rome and Armenia would have hammered out a sensible compromise, there would have been no war, and Mithradates would have died of old age in some pleasant but remote hunting-lodge.

Unfortunately young Appius Claudius, determined to seize the chance of his brother-in-law's command in the east to make his mark in great affairs, thought it would be amusing for his companions, and salutary for the Armenians, if he treated King Tigranes to a display of free-speaking republican independence. The King kept altogether too much state; he needed to be reminded that no barbarian potentate was the equal of a Roman noble.

Claudius would not follow the road by which his Armenian escort wished to take him to the Great King. After a few days in the mountains he doubled back over the Euphrates and proceeded independently to Antioch; that was the greatest city within the dominions of Tigranes, where he was sure to turn up sooner or later. The Great King was at that time campaigning in Phoenicia, so that the escort who wished to take Claudius through the Armenian hill-country were certainly wasting his time. But to journey directly to Antioch was to remind Tigranes that his wealthiest city was within easy reach of the Roman army in Cilicia; it may well have been seen by the Armenians as a veiled threat as well as a piece of bad manners.

When the Great King returned to Antioch he received the Roman embassy in all the pomp of a state audience; before his throne stood four client-Kings, their hands clasped in token of servitude. Claudius remarked to his suite that it must be twenty-five years since Tigranes had heard a free man speak his mind, and that a renewal of the experience must surely be good for his character. He then publicly announced that he brought an ultimatum: either the Great King would at once hand over Mithradates, in chains, to answer for his crimes before a Roman tribunal, or Rome would make war on him.

If Tigranes had acceded to so brusque a demand so brusquely expressed he would have impaired the prestige which was his greatest asset. In public audience he was bound to refuse, though he tried to indicate that the question was not finally closed by sending magnificent presents to the lodgings of the embassy. Claudius chose to regard these courtesies as an attempt to bribe him. He returned the presents and himself went back to Cilicia, having demonstrated his fearless republican spirit by bringing about a quite unnecessary war.

 During the autumn of 70 Lucullus was occupied in settling the government of Asia. By the opening of the new year he considered his conquests so thoroughly subdued that one legion, commanded by his legate Sornatius, would be garrison enough for Pontus. The other two provinces, Pergamum and Bithynia, were held by a legion apiece; these were probably the Fimbrian legions, which are not mentioned by name in the accounts of the Armenian war. In Asia, which for so many years had been their home, the Fimbrians would be fairly happy; they were war-weary elderly men, politically opposed to their general, and in a further campaign of conquest they would be inclined to mutiny.

That left only two legions for the invasion of Armenia, whereas five had not been considered too many for the conquest of the much smaller Kingdom of Pontus; and even with these five Lucullus had not dared to accept battle in the plain when he lay encamped beside Mithradates at Cabira. But that was eighteen months ago. Since then Lucullus had seen the Pontic army dissolve in panic when ordered to carry out an ordinary routine manœuvre, a retirement in face of the enemy. He had the measure of these Asiatic hordes, and did not fear them. With his two legions, about 10,000 foot in all, and 3,000 mercenary horse, he set out for the crossings of the Euphrates.

In Rome the democratic orators were attacking this blood-thirsty warmonger, this proud aristocrat who invaded a neighbouring Kingdom, without warrant from the Senate, merely to prolong his period of command. The legionaries also were doubtful; not because they held the war to be unrighteous but because they feared the odds were too great. It was very lucky for Lucullus that his march began with favourable omens, which could not fail to encourage nervous troops.

He found the upper Euphrates unfordable, swollen by winter rains. He therefore encamped and began to look for boats, planning to build a floating bridge. That very evening the river fell, until by next day islands were showing in midstream which normally did not appear until the dry season of summer. Without serious trouble the Romans splashed through shallow fords.

The district beyond the river was inhabited by worshippers of sacred cows. The beasts wandered about unharmed, grazing in any field that pleased them, until they were wanted for sacrifice. (Long ago the Hurrians of Mesopotamia had worshipped gods who bore Sanskrit names, and a stray tribe of Aryans must still have been settled by the banks of the Euphrates in the first century.) A Roman foraging party found one of these dedicated animals waiting placidly beside a sacrificial altar. It stood obligingly still until Lucullus could sacrifice it to Artemis, in gratitude for such an easy passage over the river. Not only were the Romans encouraged, but the local inhabitants, seeing that these strangers enjoyed the favour of heaven, decided to remain neutral.

During the past winter Tigranes had begun to regret the outburst of bad temper which had brought about this dangerous and unnecessary war. Since it is self-evident that the King of Kings cannot make a political mistake, the trouble had obviously been caused by the incompetence of his ministers. He was still not quite sure that he would support his father-in-law through thick and thin; so he did not invite him to court and give him the full state of a royal ally. In a private interview the two monarchs went through the list of their principal advisers; and several cunning but self-satisfied Greek adventurers were quietly put away by the barbarian masters from whom they had expected to make a fortune.

Tigranes told himself comfortingly that the rude young Roman whippersnapper was not important enough to commit Lucullus to a desperate war. He had gone away breathing threats, but no invasion would follow. Because events just may not happen when a Great King says they will not, he hanged the first messengers who brought him tidings of the Roman invasion. He reminded his courtiers that he could muster an army of 300,000 men; they replied that Lucullus would not dare to defend even Ephesus if the Armenians chose to march westward.

In the end a gallant soldier named Mithrobarzanes dared to tell his lord that the Roman army had crossed not only the Euphrates but the Tigris; it was nearing the new city of Tigranocerta, founded by the Great King as a tribute to his own greatness. For a moment it was touch and go, but Mithrobarzanes was not hustled out to instant execution; instead he was given a few thousand horse, and ordered to destroy the invaders. When he dispersed the Roman army he must take care to capture Lucullus alive, for the Great King wished to see him.

Mithrobarzanes was a brave man, brave enough to blurt out unpleasant truths in the Great King's audience-chamber. He led the hopeless charge of his cavalry, and was killed before the few survivors scattered in flight. At last Tigranes understood that even Tigranocerta was in danger—and he had not even begun to call out the levy of Armenia. He fled northwards from his gimcrack capital, to set up his standard among the mountains of Taurus. There the barons of Armenia could join him in safety, without venturing into the plain dominated by Roman foot.

With a rashness that was in itself an insult to the Great King Lucullus divided his small army. Murena hurried north behind Tigranes, overtook him in a defile, scattered his bodyguard and plundered his baggage; Sextilius advanced into the desert of Mesopotamia, to defeat some faint-hearted Arab chieftains who were going through the motions of rallying to their overlord. When these detachments had rejoined the main body Lucullus sat down before Tigranocerta.

That populous new foundation was defended by a wall sixty cubits in height; it contained splendid buildings, the royal harem, and much of the royal treasure. But nearly all of its 300,000 inhabitants were captives dragged from their homes in Persia or Cappadocia, unwilling settlers who could not be trusted to defend their prison. The garrison, commanded by an Armenian named Mancaeus, was made up partly of faithful Armenians and partly of Greek mercenaries; there were barely enough men to hold the long circuit of wall, and the King's magnificent hunting-palace in the suburbs must be abandoned to the besiegers.

Lucullus also stretched his little army to its limit, digging a line of trenches right round the city before he settled down to burrow mines and cast stones from his engines. So lightly held was the besieging line that a force of Armenian cavalry broke through into the city, and then fought their way out again with the harem of the Great King.

In Taurus the grand army of Armenia was mustering, to the number of 250,000 foot and 55,000 horse; many were mercenaries from foreign parts, but among them were 17,000 Armenian *cataphractarii*, horsemen as heavily armoured as any hoplite. When this great army marched down from the mountains it would interpose between the Romans and their base in Cilicia.

At last Mithradates was admitted to the presence of his host. The veteran, now approaching his sixty-third birthday, proposed to destroy Lucullus without the hazard of a pitched battle. The Armenian cavalry must command the open country; they could hem in the Roman foragers until the invaders began to starve. It would be most satisfying if Lucullus could be defeated by the tactics which he himself had employed to defeat Mithradates outside Cyzicus three years ago.

Tigranes, the type of the ruler corrupted absolutely by absolute power, resented this advice, with its implied suggestion that the Romans might beat his great army in the open field. Taxiles, a Pontic general who spoke in favour of his lord's plan of campaign, was very nearly put to death. The suspicious

The Exile

tyrant proclaimed that Mithradates, jealous of his glory, wished to cheat him of the honour of destroying a Roman consular army. When this tantrum had been cleared up it was agreed that Taxiles should remain at Armenian headquarters to give expert advice on Roman tactics; but that Mithradates should stay behind to train recruits as they came in.

At last Tigranes and his great army were in position among the foothills, overlooking the Roman camp in the plain below. Lucullus had opened his campaign in the early spring; but he had marched a very long way, and the muster of the whole levy of Armenia had been a very slow business. Our authorities are often most vexingly vague about the passage of time, but we happen to know that the great battle outside Tigranocerta was fought on the 6th of October. That was supposed to be an unlucky day for the Roman army, for it was the anniversary of a great defeat. When Lucullus was reminded of this he answered cheerfully that in future the day would be considered a lucky one.

That was at a council of war, held at Roman headquarters on the 5th. Some officers advised Lucullus to cling to his trenches, where the Armenian cavalry could not easily charge his foot; others suggested that he should abandon the siege, and march out with all his men to meet the Great King in open battle. In the same confident spirit Lucullus summed up; he said that he had heard a great deal of good advice, and would follow all of it. He would march against the Great King, but he would also cling to his trenches. Murena was detached with a small force to occupy the lines of investment, while Lucullus marched against the Great King with less than 10,000 legionaries and a handful of horse. He was challenging odds of 25 to 1, and he knew it; but since he had driven Mithradates from Pontus be believed that Roman legionaries were superior to any number of undrilled Asiatics.

As he looked down at the camp of his adversaries Tigranes made an observation which posterity has remembered: 'If these men have come as an embassy they are too many; but if they come as an army they are too few.' His Armenian officers fell to gambling for their share of the spoil that must be taken next day, and grumbled that here was no work for so many men. Each came individually to Tigranes and offered to destroy the

144

The Exile

Romans with his own command, if as reward he might have all the plunder of their camp. Only Taxiles was doubtful. He maintained that the Romans would come out to fight, and that the Great King would need every man he could put in line.

On the morning of the 6th the Armenian leaders, watching from high ground, saw the Romans on the move. A river ran between the two armies, and when the Romans began to march towards the nearest ford it looked at first as though they were retreating. Tigranes of course was jubilant. Taxiles pointed out that Romans setting out on a long march carried corselet and shield slung in a bundle on their backs; these men wore full armour, without even the usual leather dust-covers which kept it clean. They were prepared for battle.

Though it was just possible that this handful of Romans might be willing to face attack, no Armenian supposed that they would take the offensive. Then an Eagle, surrounded by its glittering escort, was seen to cross the ford and advance towards the hill; and there was Lucullus, to be recognized by his purple cloak, marching stolidly at the head of his men with his sword bare in his hand. A commander-in-chief would only dismount and draw his sword as the signal for immediate all-out attack. The Armenians had taken it for granted that it would be for them to do the attacking when they were quite ready for it, and they were not yet properly arrayed. Tigranes grew flustered as he saw time running out before he was ready for battle. He could not issue coherent orders, but merely gasped: 'What, do *they* attack *us*?' His men jostled into their accustomed ranks. But the units were crowded too closely together, and none of the divisional generals knew what he was supposed to be doing.

The striking-force of the Armenian host was the corps of 17,000 *cataphractarii*, lancers clothed in complete mail. These men had been trained to charge against the phalanx; they themselves fell in as a phalanx on horseback, the long barge-poles of their lances threaded between the files to project in front. Had there been time they might have been ordered to draw out in line; but this unexpected Roman offensive meant that there was no time for manœuvre. The clumsy column of lancers, all facing to the front, was thrown into disorder by the charge of a small number of Galatian horse who galloped round to take

K   145

them in flank. Lucullus, with only two cohorts behind him, cut straight through the Armenian foot and rallied his men on a hillock in rear of the enemy. Then he turned his small force, perhaps 1,000 infantry, against the rear of the Armenian cavalry. The horsemen panicked, and in their flight rode over their own foot. The front ranks of the infantry turned to flee, to find their way blocked by dense masses of reserves. The legions ran in to complete the slaughter.

Before the battle Lucullus had issued stringent orders forbidding plunder while there was an enemy in the field; and consciousness of their desperate situation made his men obey him, as they had not obeyed him at the capture of Amisus and Sinope. The pursuit had been pressed for fifteen miles before the Romans, exhausted, returned to rob the slain. It was said that 100,000 barbarians fell, and five Romans. Certainly a victory against such great odds had never been known in the previous history of the City.

The Great King had been among the first to flee, and because he was well mounted he got clear away. None the less, he was in a state of abject terror. Seeing one of his sons riding near by he pressed his imperial diadem on the young man. The prince, fearing that later he might be accused of treason, refused the dangerous honour. But he dared not hand it back; he passed it on to one of his slaves, who in equal terror threw it away. Later it was found by a Roman, who presented it to Lucullus.

One of the qualities that made Lucullus a great soldier was his unexpectedness; the enemy never knew what he would do next. He had earned a reputation for caution when he starved out the Pontic besiegers of Cyzicus, refusing battle though his army was eager to fight; now, when delay might have starved out the enemy, he attacked suddenly in the face of amazing odds, and by sheer speed of movement snatched an unbelievable victory.

Mancaeus, the commandant in Tigranocerta, had seen the rout of the royal army and knew that he would not be relieved. He knew also that after such a disaster his Greek mercenaries would be eager to make terms with the victor. Since he was a loyal servant of his King and determined on a stout defence he at once disarmed the Greeks; but he scrupled to kill them merely as a precaution, before they had openly turned against him. In this kind of warfare there was no room for scruple. The disarmed Greeks banded themselves together, seized clubs for weapons and wrapped cloaks round their left arms for shields; then they attacked a section of the wall from within, and as soon as they had won the battlements invited the Romans to enter.

The army of the Great King was made up of contingents from many races. The mountaineers of Armenia, like their cousins from Cappadocia and Persia, were willing to fight man to man against Europeans; but Syrians and Mesopotamians are feeble cattle, to be chased in crowds by any warrior who will put on a brave front, and the Arabs of the desert think only of joining the winning side. All the same, the fall of Tigranocerta was a striking example of the ascendancy of disarmed westerners over armed but cringing Asiatics.

Within the city the Romans took an immense plunder, so valuable that the delighted troops were easily persuaded to refrain from massacre. Lucullus was at pains to conciliate the unfortunate citizens, who had first been dragged by force to this alien settlement and then robbed of all they possessed because the tyrant who had uprooted them could not defend his capital. From the booty it was easy to spare them a pittance for journey-money; they were dismissed to their original homes, in Greek Asia or on the far side of Mesopotamia. But first was held a little ceremony which must have given great pleasure to the cultured Lucullus. The magnificent theatre of Tigranocerta had been completed just before the siege began, and the company of actors engaged for the opening performance had actually been caught inside the town. In the presence of the Roman army the curtain rose on a short season of Greek plays. Then the whole magnificent foundation, city, theatre, palace and suburbs, was left desolate. Tigranocerta flourished for less than a single lifetime, and then vanished so completely that at the present day archaeologists are not agreed on its site.

The chieftains who had been conquered by Tigranes revolted as soon as they learned that their conqueror had been defeated. King Zarbienus of Gordiene had the bad luck to be held hostage in Armenia when his army went over to the Romans; Lucullus found his corpse, and gave him a splendid funeral in his own city. The King of Sophene, and other chieftains of the

Arabs, sent contingents of horse to serve with the Roman army.

The King of the Parthians sent an embassy to open friendly relations with the new power which had arisen on his western border. The Parthians were nomad horse-archers from the steppe beyond the Caspian. They had recently overrun Persia; now they were expanding cautiously in every direction, demanding tribute from their weaker neighbours and recoiling from any people who stood up to their threats.

The Parthian King pursued the obvious but not very intelligent diplomatic policy which would occur to any vigorous savage. If the Romans would permit him to conquer Mesopotamia and recognize him as its rightful ruler, he would help them against the Armenians. In itself that was a reasonable proposal, though after this great victory Lucullus was not especially in need of allies. The Parthians spoiled the effect of this reasonable behaviour by making exactly the same offer, in the same terms, to King Tigranes.

Of course news of this double-dealing was quickly carried to Lucullus. He chose to be angry at what was no more than an example of the standard diplomatic practice of the orient, dismissed the Parthian envoys from his headquarters, and threatened that next spring he would march into their land; for it was already November, and time to go into winter quarters.

The lateness of the season afforded King Tigranes another chance. As he galloped in panic from the rout of his army he had encountered a small contingent of allies, well-trained horsemen of high morale. Mithradates had with him the exiled vassals of Pontus, gallant Persians who remained faithful to their hereditary chieftain; he had also the servants and camp furniture appropriate to his royal rank. When the fleeing Tigranes had dined once more in kingly state he recovered his courage. The two Kings sat down together to salvage what they could from the lost campaign.

As Great King, King of Kings, Tigranes had shown himself petulant and incompetent. But in his youth he had fought his way through the jungle of treasons and assassination plots which was the domestic life of every Hellenistic royal family, and later he had conquered Syria and Mesopotamia. In adversity he became once more a tough and wily Armenian warrior. Romans might mock at these oriental Kings, too vain to hear bad news, softened with luxury, cruel, faithless and avaricious; but each individual who sat securely on a throne had reached it only after a fierce struggle with his nearest relatives. Mithradates at the beginning of his career had been compelled to imprison his mother, and to kill his brother and his sister-wife. No one reproached him for these deeds, which were the usual accompaniment of the struggle for supremacy. Every eastern ruler must be at bottom brave, energetic, and ingenious; otherwise he would cease to rule.

Tigranes had the winter in which to gather another army. Luckily there was at his court a superb military administrator, a ruler who had twice astonished his enemies by raising great armies out of nothing. Tigranes showed wisdom and self-restraint in putting all the resources of his Kingdom at the disposal of Mithradates, who magnanimously overlooked the shabby treatment he had received when he first fled into exile. During that winter of 69–68 Mithradates and Tigranes showed what oriental Kings could do, when they knew that their thrones and their heads were at stake.

The glens of warlike Armenia, the hereditary realm of Tigranes, had not hitherto been touched by the Roman invasion. The King's first action was to summon to his standard every Armenian capable of bearing arms. When this throng of mountaineers was assembled Mithradates took charge, and what he did with them demonstrates the independence of his judgement. In his opinion numbers were not everything. At Tigranocerta the Romans had been victorious against odds of 25 to 1; in 87 and 74 the great Pontic hosts who had marched against them had met shattering defeat. In the barren country of Armenia it would be difficult to feed a large army; and many poor mountaineers, though personally brave, had come to the muster with no weapon save a knife. Mithradates therefore selected 70,000 of the stoutest foot, and dismissed the rest to their homes. Armenia bordered on the land of the Chalybes, where iron had first been smelted into swords; it would be the duty of these superfluous soldiers to make weapons and armour for their comrades in the front line.

But in a war against Romans, who themselves employed only second-rate mercenary horse, every mounted man had his value. Of the Armenian cavalry no less than 35,000 were

retained under arms, which must have been the full levy of
horse in the country. The result was an army of a composition
strange to antiquity, in which cavalry made up one-third of the
total force. Perhaps Mithradates was planning to try out a new
tactical doctrine, an anticipation of the mounted warfare of the
Middle Ages.

Meanwhile these chosen troops must be drilled as well as
armed. In keeping with his new theory, of a small army of first-
class troops rather than weight of untrained numbers, Mithradates handed over the training to the Roman exiles who had
accompanied him from Pontus. The foot were divided into
cohorts, and practised in the Roman methods of swift deploy-
ment and fast movement over broken ground.

About the beginning of this winter of mobilization and training Mithradates celebrated his sixty-third birthday. Even by
the generous standards which are applied to Kings he was well
past the age of military service.

We are inclined to see armed opposition to Rome as a gallant
but hopeless struggle; we forget, as the Romans themselves
forgot, how often, from Scotland to Arabia, Roman armies invaded a country and then withdrew, baffled. In the spring of
68 it seemed for a time that Tigranes had achieved the freedom
of his country. Lucullus had decided that the barren mountains
of Armenia were a less worthy prize than the great Mesopo-
tamian cities which paid tribute to the Parthians. The double-
dealing of the Parthian King gave him a just cause for war, and
he could argue plausibly that if he marched victorious into
Persia the few dissidents who still held out in Pontus and
Armenia would be cowed into seeking peace. His real motive
was probably the love of adventure and a desire for immortal
fame. After that glorious victory outside Tigranocerta he
thought with reason that a Roman army could defeat any foe;
and it was impossible for a general to campaign in Syria, surrounded by Greek flatterers, without continually being reminded of the exploits of Alexander.

Lucullus therefore prepared for a march to the east, and sent
word to the legions in Pontus and Bithynia that they were to
join him for a campaign which would add to the Roman
dominions lands previously unknown even to geographers.

The Exile

The Fimbrians were living comfortably in a wealthy and civilized land; at the same time they could take pride in their arduous foreign service, far in front of what had been until recently the frontier of Rome. They were reluctant to travel through the unknown deserts beyond the Tigris, and the Parthians were said to be most dangerous foes. (As a matter of fact they destroyed the first Roman army which marched against them, slew Crassus the Triumvir, and maintained their independence until, some centuries later, they were supplanted by a dynasty of native Persians.) It was not even necessary for the Fimbrians to plead prudence, which their opponents might have stigmatized as cowardice; they had a plausible patriotic catchword. Up in the hills of Armenia was Mithradates, guilty of the slaughter of 80,000 unarmed Italians; his crime had gone unpunished for just on twenty years. It was the first duty of every loyal Roman to pursue him, if necessary to the edge of the known world.

The garrisons in Asia announced that they would not cross the Tigris, though to the invasion of Armenia they would march willingly. Their officers agreed to the compromise; when these gallant legionaries reached home they would have votes, and Roman domestic politics were then in a very unsettled condition. Lucullus himself nursed political ambitions; but a general who drove his army to mutiny would be disgraced in Rome, while the conqueror who displayed the captive Mithradates in his Triumph might very probably be rewarded with another consulship. Yielding to the pressure of his unruly soldiers, he prepared to march north to Armenia instead of east to Persepolis.

By this time the season was well advanced. Armenia was known to be a barren land, where feeding an army would be difficult. Lucullus therefore delayed until the barley was ripe; then he marched over Taurus, reckoning to supply his men with grain gathered from the fields as he advanced through hostile territory.

But the uplands of Armenia did not enjoy the climate of the hot Syrian plain; on the plateau the barley was still green and uneatable. The Romans were in danger of starvation; until they were saved, ironically, by the prudent forethought of Mithradates. With great pains the exiled King had stored up the whole harvest of the previous year, so that as his army manœuvred it might draw supplies from any quarter. But since Tigranes now insisted on concentrating all his forces for the defence of his capital, the city of Artaxata, Lucullus was able to pillage the undefended depots on his line of march.

The Armenians were unnerved by the contemplation of their own temerity. Here was the invincible Roman army, marching straight on their capital city. They were committed to meeting it in a pitched battle. As the crisis approached they grew more and more jumpy. Tigranes shared the feelings of his followers; from day to day he put off the final test, until the Romans had reached the neighbourhood of Artaxata. Inside this small but strongly fortified city were the royal harem and the royal treasure; for its impregnable walls were said to have been designed by the great Hannibal, once an exile given refuge at the Armenian court. Its loss would be an irreparable disaster; yet it could only be saved by the hazard of a battle.

The accounts of what followed are confused, as confused as the councils of the defenders; for it seems evident that Tigranes was reluctant to fight, while Mithradates urged him to the gamble of a decisive encounter. At first the Armenians tried to delay the Roman advance by digging field-works; at the last minute they shrank from trench-warfare at close quarters, and shut themselves up in their fortified camp. When Lucullus tried to lure them into open battle they remained behind their palisade. Presently the Armenian cavalry came out, without their foot, in the hope of surprising the Roman vanguard on the march. But the troopers broke disgracefully even before they reached the Roman column; many of them rode straight home, to take no further part in the war. Seeing his common troopers panic, Tigranes put himself at the head of the Satrapeni, the nobles and their household men. Even these were defeated by the few mercenary horse in Roman service, and both Tigranes and Mithradates galloped from the field while the battle still raged. That some Armenian nobles fought gallantly is shown by a passage quoted in Plutarch from a lost book of Livy; Lucullus reported to the Senate that though outside Tigranocerta he had killed a larger total of the enemy, outside Artaxata the Armenians lost more of their chieftains and senior officers.

When all seemed lost the independence of Armenia was

saved by her savage climate. After drinking the icy water of the glacier-streams the Romans and their baggage-animals suffered from colic; and that year the snow-storms of winter began in September. Lucullus begged his men to persevere, that they might have the glory of capturing fortifications designed by the great Hannibal; but soldiers from central Italy could not endure snow at harvest time. To avert a mutiny Lucullus turned his back on untaken Artaxata; he returned to the lowlands of Syria by another route, to avoid the disgrace of retracing his steps.

The Romans came down into the plain in the neighbourhood of Nisibis, a city to the east of the Euphrates still occupied by the troops of Tigranes. This last Armenian foothold in the plain was commanded by the King's brother Gouras; his chief engineer was a Greek named Callimachus, who had been expert adviser to the defenders of Amisus in the siege of 72–70.

The Romans at once sat down to besiege Nisibis, for the mild winter of Syria need not put a stop to campaigning. Since Tigranes dared not advance with an army of relief the siege could have only one end. When the battering had gone far enough Lucullus ordered an assault, which was successful. Prince Gouras was treated with kindness; but for Callimachus there was no mercy. Ostensibly he was executed because he had burned Amisus rather than yield it, and thus deprived Lucullus of an opportunity of showing clemency to the vanquished. But of course his real crime was that he knew more about siege-craft than anyone in the Roman army. In antiquity a brave defence was usually punished with death; quarter was the reward of cowardice or inefficiency. It is hard for us to dismiss from our minds a thousand years of Christian chivalry, and to see, as a Roman saw, that the braver the foe the more necessary it is to kill him.

After the capture of Nisibis it seemed that Lucullus was free to march where he would. He might continue eastward and overthrow the Parthians; he might take over southern Syria, Palestine and Phoenicia, left masterless by the defeat of Tigranes; he might, as soon as the thaw came, return to Armenia and once again form the siege of Artaxata.

Suddenly, when there was not an enemy in the field, he found himself helpless. His army refused to follow him. For more than sixty years the civil wars had been eating away the famous Roman discipline. Soldiers who are led in rebellion against the state must always feel in their hearts the possibility of rebellion against their military superiors; in particular the Fimbrians had volunteered to fight for democracy and by force of circumstance had found themselves for the last fifteen years serving under one eminent oligarch after another. But the personal failings of Lucullus reinforced the urge to mutiny.

His greatest fault in Roman eyes was that he habitually put the welfare of provincials before the comfort of his own troops. He knew that Roman soldiers, admitted within the walls of an unarmed city, would rob and mistreat the citizens they were supposed to protect. Therefore during all the years that he campaigned in Asia he made his men pass the winter in hutted camps, instead of among the baths and theatres and brothels of the great Greek-founded towns. He enforced rigorous discipline, and made his men live simply. Soldiers sometimes glory in the hardness of their lot, boasting that in this tough army no one sleeps in a bed or eats a cooked meal; but that happens only when they can see their commander sharing their privations. By Roman standards Lucullus was personally disinterested; though he managed during a career of active service to amass a great fortune. But he was in love with Greek refinement, which seemed to Italian peasants to be unmanly luxury. It was no use the commander sharing the sour wine and cold porridge of his men, if he drank from a chased silver goblet and ate with a golden spoon. Perhaps he also passed the winter in an unheated camp; but his hut was hung with purple and his bed was a work of art. Any Greek who complained that he had been robbed by a soldier was sure of a hearing; an honest legionary who had been cheated by foreigners dared not stand up for his rights. The soldiers knew also, for they were voters who kept in touch with home affairs, that in the Forum all the demagogues of the Popular party were hunting Lucullus. In speech after speech he was denounced as a greedy aristocrat, who feathered his own nest while exposing honest Romans to unnecessary hardship. He demanded perpetual extensions of what was in theory an annual command, on the pretext that the enemies of Rome were still unconquered; when in fact he was making war on harmless strangers at his own whim, without the warrant of the Senate. At any moment a resolution might pass the Assembly, depriving him of his office. When his successor came out Lucullus might try to avoid him by marching into unknown country; unless his troops, true guardians of the constitution, kept him in the camp outside Nisibis where messengers could find him.

In the camp Claudius was preaching the duty of disobedience to his commander and brother-in-law. He himself had brought about the war with Tigranes by his arrogance and lack of tact; but that was no reason why he should not denounce it as another example of the boundless ambition of Lucullus. The general was reluctant to punish his kinsman. The soldiers listened, and agreed with what they heard. Soon it was impossible to make them do anything, except wait where they were until further orders came from Rome.

During the winter of 68–67 Tigranes and Mithradates could refit and recuperate, secure in the knowledge that no enemy could approach before the snow was off the passes. They knew also, for the Roman exiles with Mithradates must have been in touch with home politics, that in the near future Lucullus would be deprived of his command. With any luck the main Roman army might go home with him, since the Senate was tired of these long wars in the east. Tigranes had decided on his future policy; he would draw in his horns and rest content with his ancestral Kingdom. There he could defend himself against Roman attack; but if the Romans would allow him to reign there undisturbed he was prepared to be a friend and ally of the Roman People. Syria and all the rest of the rich unwarlike south might remain in the possession of the invaders. His born subjects, tough hillmen, would fight for Armenia; they could not defend the hot plains against those terrible legions.

All the same, there could be no peace while Lucullus commanded an army. Submission and the offer of alliance must wait until his successor appeared. Just to prove that the east was still unconquered, to make the Romans pause before they invaded Armenia for a second time, there would be no harm in stirring up more trouble for them in the districts they had already won.

So Mithradates, that helpless exile dependent on Armenian

bounty, was lent 4,000 Armenian foot; with these men, and another 4,000 Pontic exiles who had rallied to him in the past year, he was despatched over the hills in the middle of winter to see how much of a nuisance he could make of himself in the valley of the Lycus. At the age of 64 the stubborn old enemy of Rome was back in Comana, the most holy shrine of Pontus. The lieutenants of Lucullus heard of his arrival; but they considered the country to be impassable in winter, and he remained undisturbed until spring should melt the snow and dry the roads.

VI

The Chieftain

During the winter of 68 it was assumed in Rome that the war against Mithradates was finished. Pontus had been conquered; the whole land was now occupied by Roman garrisons, the old King had fled into helpless exile at the court of defeated Armenia. What exercised the statesmen in the Senate was not the need for further victories, but the difficulty of achieving peace. So long as Lucullus marched about the orient at the head of a great army he would always find another foe to fight, merely to safeguard his position as proconsul in command of the principal force in Roman service. His own men had frustrated his ambitious plan for the conquest of Parthia; but trouble would continue while he had legions under his orders. Lucullus must go. Then there would be peace in Asia.

The proconsular command in the east was now the greatest prize in Roman political life. The rebellion in Spain had been quelled by Pompeius; for the present the Gauls were quiet. Nowhere else was there a Roman army on a war footing, whose leader could hope to be rewarded with a Triumph after a year or so of active service. In addition, the establishment of a permanent civil administration for the new province of Pontus ought to provide massive bribes for the Senatorial commissioners who would fix the amount of tribute to be paid by each city for centuries to come; and there would be comfortable well-paid posts for the dependants whom they would leave in Asia as petty officials.

Ever since the death of Sulla the nobility had controlled the Senate; and the firmest conviction of the nobility was that, while all nobles were very much better and more important than common citizens, each noble was the equal of every other

157

The Chieftain

noble. Putting this principle into effect, the Senate appointed as the new governor of Asia the noble next in line for a job, the undistinguished Manius Acilius Glabrio, a consul for that year. In late autumn a message was despatched to Lucullus in Syria, to inform him that his successor would be arriving in the spring. Glabrio would be accompanied by the usual commission of Senators. Until these men arrived Lucullus was forbidden to initiate any new line of policy. In fear that the ambitious commander might begin another war before he was relieved this news was also conveyed to his army.

But the Popular party was reviving; especially now that Pompeius, once a favourite of Sulla, had changed sides and put himself at the head of the opposition. The Populars recognized that a mob cannot govern; they hoped to overthrow the nobility by putting extraordinary unconstitutional power in the hands of a Popular leader. It so happened that there was a very good excuse for a temporary extraordinary command. The pirates had recently grown so strong that they interfered with all sea-borne trade, and even hampered the vital movement of African corn to Rome; they had taken to raiding isolated stretches of road on the shore of Italy itself, and had carried off for ransom some high officials of the government.

Having conquered Spain Pompeius must disband his army. He wanted command of the only other Roman army on active service; the Popular politicians were willing to support him. But such a scheme had no particular appeal for the mob, which was clamouring for action against the pirates. There were stormy scenes in the Forum, until eventually an extraordinary law was carried by the open threat of renewed civil war: Pompeius was to have a special command against the pirates, instead of the command against Mithradates which was what he really wanted; but the terms of this command were so wide that in fact all the soldiers and ships of Rome anywhere in the world could be put at his disposal. In every province which bordered on the sea (that is, every province of any importance) Pompeius would rank with but before its constitutional governor; all clients and allies were ordered to support him; his term of office was to be a minimum of three years, instead of the customary annual command which could only be renewed by a special decree of the Senate.

The Chieftain

Glabrio had reached Bithynia when he learned of these developments at home. There seemed to be no point in going any further, for by the time he reached Syria to supersede Lucullus, Pompeius would be on his way to supersede him. He was nominally proconsul in Bithynia, as well as commander of the army which must suppress Mithradates. He remained in his province which after all must have needed someone to govern it.

Thus during the campaigning season of 67 the eastern army of Rome was immobilized. Lucullus in Syria was forbidden to start a new campaign, and was aware that as soon as his successor arrived he would have to hand over his command. His men knew this also, and if he had ordered them to march they would not have obeyed him. Glabrio refused to risk defeat, when if he gained a victory Pompeius would reap the glory. Pompeius was busy with the pirates.

Mithradates, surrounded by Roman exiles, knew all that happened in the Forum. The little army which he had led to Comana had been granted one season in which to reconquer Pontus; in the following year Pompeius would arrive, a famous soldier with an army even stronger than that which had followed Sulla to the siege of Piraeus. But if he found the King of Pontus once more firmly established on his throne he might recognize the accomplished fact rather than begin again the long wars from the very beginning. In this one year Mithradates must drive out the invaders.

He marched first against Fabius, who lay encamped with one legion in the valley of Cabira, scene of the panic which had given Pontus to the Romans. He advanced boldly, and Fabius drew out his men in line of battle to meet the challenge. The conflict lasted all day, until in the evening Fabius fell back on his fortified camp. The Romans had not been broken; but they had been worsted, with heavy casualties. Fabius recognized that his situation was desperate.

With a force composed, after the usual Roman fashion, of sound heavy infantry and a few unreliable mercenary horse he had been caught in the wide valley which Mithradates, who knew the country thoroughly, had picked five years ago as ideally suited to cavalry action. He dared not form his men in column of route in face of the Pontic horse; and though his camp was too strongly fortified to be taken by assault he had

The Chieftain

not stores enough to face a siege. All he could do was to offer battle on the next day, in the hope that his well-drilled legions would scatter the rebel levies.

There was very little hope, and Fabius knew it. Before offering battle on the second day he was reduced to an expedient unique in Roman military history: he freed all the slaves in his camp, armed them, and put them in the fighting line. Evidently he thought himself to be enormously outnumbered, although in the previous autumn Mithradates had returned to his Kingdom with a total force of 8,000 men; the mountaineers of inner Pontus must have swarmed out of their castles to rally round the standard of their ancient dynasty.

The second day's battle was long and fierce; but in the end the Romans were once more driven back. They were losing their formation, and the retreat was becoming a rout, when an accident brought the action to a premature close. As Mithradates led his cavalry in the decisive charge he suddenly fell from his horse, wounded in the knee by a slingstone, and in the face by a javelin.

It is an astonishing picture. In his youth the absolute and luxurious King feasted in Pergamum while his soldiers fought for him in Boeotia; war was beneath his dignity, and his person too precious to be endangered. In middle age he commanded armies, but there is no record that he fought in person. Now, in his sixty-fifth year, he charged at the head of his troops. Anyone who was present at a battle might be hit by a slingstone, for the sling was a weapon of long range; but the Roman javelin was thrown only just before the swords crossed. It is as though a modern commander-in-chief were to be wounded, not by a rifle, but by a revolver.

It is perhaps not so surprising to find that his soldiers were devoted to their gallant old commander. As soon as he was seen to fall the charge faltered. When he was carried back to his tent the whole army marched with him, and Fabius withdrew unmolested to the protection of his palisade. But still he dared not retreat down the open valley, where Pontic horse could charge his marching column. He clung to his position, all the more stubbornly because he had news that Triarius, commander of the whole garrison in Roman Asia, was marching to reinforce him.

The Chieftain

For a few days Mithradates hovered between life and death, amid the grief and dismay of his army. Once he had turned the corner he made a quick recovery, thanks to the eccentric medical treatment administered by his personal physicians. Throughout his long career the King displayed a deep interest in poison, and especially in antidotes to poison; he still took his daily dose of 'the antidote', the specific against all poisons, which long ago had preserved his health from the intrigues of his mother. He kept in his household certain wise men of the Scythian tribe of the Agari, who employed the venom of serpents as a remedy for wounds. Under this drastic régime his injuries were quickly healed, and he was soon in the saddle again.

A few days later Triarius reached Cabira. As senior to Fabius he took over the command, and the united Roman army was now strong enough to march through open country. Triarius withdrew cautiously towards the south-west, intending to fall back on Deiotarus and his Galatian warriors. It seems odd that in this war neither side made any use of the sea. Perhaps every available Roman warship had been collected into the great fleet with which Pompeius was crushing the pirates; and of course the pirates themselves would be too busy to help Mithradates. The natural Roman line of retreat would have been northward to the coast; but if there were no ships in the Euxine Galatia was also a convenient refuge.

As the Romans retired Mithradates advanced; but he did not consider himself strong enough to attack, and his movement could not be described as a pursuit. All the same Triarius, who found it very galling to be followed in this way, was eager to wipe out the shame at the earliest opportunity. He was still among the central mountains, near a little town named Zela, when a report reached him that Lucullus was marching westward. The report was in fact untrue; Lucullus, at the mercy of mutinous troops, was in no condition to march anywhere. But it tempted Triarius to try his luck once again. If Lucullus was approaching, Mithradates must detach troops to face him; therefore the Pontic army ought to be weaker than it had been at Cabira. To an ambitious Roman legate it was even more important that the arrival of the proconsul would end his tenure of an independent command. If Triarius wished to be hailed as

The Chieftain

Imperator by victorious legions, and such was the highest ambition of every Roman general, he must fight quickly before he was superseded.

Suddenly, therefore, at Zela the Romans turned about and took the offensive. Mithradates proved equal to the occasion. Once more he fought all day in the front rank, until after hours of bitter struggle the division under his personal command was the first to press back the Roman line. The invincible legionaries, the best infantry in the world, gave ground until they became entangled in a deep and muddy ditch. There they lost formation. For the first and last time in these long wars (for the army of Nudus at Chalcedon had been composed chiefly of Greek auxiliaries) Mithradates saw regular Roman foot flee before him.

When the infantry had been overthrown Mithradates led his men against the mercenary cavalry in Roman service. If these also could be broken the Romans would have no rearguard; their whole army might be butchered to the last man.

The King was foremost in the pursuit. Since he was well into his sixty-fifth year and only just recovered from two serious wounds he was of course mounted, though he was leading his foot. As he trotted forward a few members of his bodyguard ran beside his horse. Thus a Roman centurion, naturally one of the last to flee, suddenly found himself running beside the King. The Popular exiles in the Pontic army fought in Roman armour, and in antiquity uniforms were unknown; the centurion realized that everyone around him had mistaken him for another member of the royal bodyguard. He edged closer, and then saw that the King's magnificent corselet was proof against any sword-stroke. He did what he could, by slashing at the old man's unarmoured thigh. Of course there was time for only one blow; then the genuine bodyguard knew him for a foe and cut him down. It was an outstandingly courageous and self-sacrificing deed, done by a Roman hero whose name unfortunately has not come down to us.

Mithradates fell fainting from the saddle, and at once his army halted in consternation. First aid was needed, rather than the venomous decoctions of the Agari. A Greek surgeon staunched the flow of blood, and after a brief rest the old King climbed once more into the saddle.

The Chieftain

But the delay had enabled the Romans to break contact. Eager to exploit his victory to the full, Mithradates at once led his men in an assault on the Roman camp; only to find that Triarius had abandoned his sick, his baggage, and all his supplies, and had left his tents standing while his routed army fled on towards Cappadocia.

In the evening Mithradates encamped on the battlefield. At his advanced age he had sustained three serious wounds in quick succession, and he was physically incapable of further pursuit. But he was to such a degree the inspiration of his men that he could not send his army on without him. Instead the Pontic soldiers employed their leisure in stripping the dead; presently they reported to headquarters a significant discovery.

The Romans had left on the field 7,000 corpses. That represented a heavy rate of casualties, though it was far from the utter annihilation which would have been their fate if Mithradates had not been put out of action by his untimely wound. But among these dead were 24 military tribunes and 150 centurions. On parade a tribune commanded at least one cohort of 600 men, a centurion was in charge of about 80 rank and file. Thus the proportion of officers killed to other ranks was nearly twice as high as it should have been. Obviously, the legionaries had fled in panic while their officers were still fighting. Here was a striking proof of the complete demoralization of excellent Roman professional soldiers.

The battle of Zela was the last encounter in the campaigning season of 67. As soon as he had lost contact with Triarius Mithradates withdrew towards Lesser Armenia, which returned to its old allegiance. But he withdrew only because, like Triarius, he believed Lucullus was approaching. When he knew for certain that the main Roman army was immobilized in Syria he returned to Pontus, occupied the whole of the inland, and advanced his posts even beyond the frontier of Cappadocia. It seems, from the silence of our authorities, that he did not attempt to reconquer the coast; while he was without a fleet Amisus and Sinope would be of no use to him.

The rejoicings at the King's return to the land of his fathers were marred by a plot at military headquarters. It was known that Pompeius would soon take command of the Roman army, and at that time Pompeius, who more than once changed parties, was reckoned to be a supporter of the Populars; certainly he owed his command to Popular votes in the Forum. It was natural that Pontic exiles in the Pontic army should explore the possibility of making peace with their countrymen. But negotiations with the enemy in the middle of a war are always a strain on good faith, and one prominent exile was tempted into treason. Attidius was discovered to be intriguing with the Romans, though it is uncertain whether he was plotting against the life of his protector or merely arranging to bring back the Pontic 'legion' to the Eagles. The measures taken by Mithradates to punish this conspiracy afford us some insight into his character.

Attidius had been a Senator when he fled from Rome, at least twenty years before his plot was discovered. (Especially under Sulla's constitution, it was possible to enter the Senate very young.) His treason deserved death, and therefore the King had him killed. But in deference to his high rank he suffered a painless military execution, and he was not tortured beforehand to make him reveal his confederates. Lesser Romans involved in the plot were tortured to the uttermost, until all had been revealed; then they also were killed, painfully and ignominiously. But the numerous servants who had taken part as messengers and go-betweens escaped scot free, whether they were slaves or freedmen. This was because, in the eyes of a Pontic chieftain, it was the duty of any lesser man to follow his lord with absolute fidelity. The fidelity of his vassals was the only foundation of the diminished power which yet remained to Mithradates; he would not weaken it by punishing vassals for loyalty even to treacherous lords.

Meanwhile the army which surrounded Lucullus (it could no longer be said that he commanded it) had drifted by slow stages from Syria to Cappadocia. The men were completely out of hand, delighting to offer insults to their unfortunate general. Lucullus impaired his dignity, the most precious possession of any Roman noble, by making personal appeals to individual mutineers; his appeals went unheeded. The soldiers had many legitimate grievances, of which the chief was their long service oversea without relief. But they knew that the blame for this lay on the Senate, not on the proconsul in nominal command; they reproached Lucullus for something which it was in his power to alter—he would not permit them to plunder the provincials.

What angered them most of all was that Lucullus had amassed a huge fortune, quite honourably by Roman standards; Greek cities gave him valuable presents in return for his lenient administration of their affairs. When he had ordered his soldiers to march to the support of Triarius they had flung empty purses at his feet, declaring that they would not fight again until these purses had been filled with plunder.

Once the whole army had been collected in Cappadocia the Fimbrians were naturally foremost in disorder. At the same time they showed a respect for the letter of army regulations which seems equally typical of the legal-minded Roman and of the experienced old soldier. They claimed that their term of enlistment would expire at the end of the current season. In the Roman army there were no long-service pensions; but every veteran who retired with an honourable discharge expected to receive a piece of land, or a good lump sum in cash, to start him in civilian life. The Fimbrians were not going to endanger their honourable discharges by open mutiny in the last months of their service. Although they refused to march, they made it clear that they were still willing to fight. At some time in the autumn, about the traditional date for going into winter quarters, they solemnly paraded in full armour, drew their swords, and charged across the empty parade-ground to the sound of the warcry. Then they disarmed, as they insisted for the last time; and reported that since there appeared to be no enemy in the field they had done their whole duty and were ready to return to Rome.

At this time, when Pontic outposts stood on Cappadocian soil and all the old Kingdom of Pontus was back under the rule of Mithradates, commissioners from the Senate arrived in the Roman camp. They pointed out that more than a year ago Lucullus had sent home an official despatch reporting the final subjugation of Pontus; therefore the Senate had commissioned them to draw up the customary allotment of revenue which was always carried out when a new province was added to the Roman dominions. The timing of their arrival must have been inspired by Popular malice. Lucullus could only reply to them that when he wrote to Rome Pontus had indeed been conquered; but that now it must be conquered all over again.

It was at once decided that Pompeius must take over the war against Mithradates, as soon as he had eliminated the pirates. Glabrio never assumed the great military command which the Senate had allotted to him, and in fact he was soon so thoroughly forgotten that some ancient historians have complicated the chronology of the war by omitting him altogether. Presently Pompeius landed in Cilicia.

The great pirate menace had collapsed as soon as the Romans took it seriously; which proves that it need never have arisen if the Senate had bothered to maintain a regular fleet. The most obvious reason for its defeat was that pirates see no profit in fighting against warships. It took Pompeius less than forty days to clear all the western basin of the Mediterranean; he merely sent squadrons of Roman warships to every pirate lair in Sicily and Corsica. Without fighting the pirates withdrew to their permanent base on the coast of Cilicia. When Pompeius with his main fleet approached Cilicia there was a kind of battle, for the great united fleet of the pirates could not surrender without striking a blow. But the crews of these pirate ships had really nothing to fight for, unless they aspired to take over the whole dominion of Rome; and few of them were so grandly ambitious. The sea-fight at Coracesium was not strenuously contested, and soon afterwards the various pirate citadels sent envoys to seek terms of peace.

Pompeius was in a hurry to finish these police-operations and get on to the war against Mithradates, in which there was glory to be won. Any pirate who would surrender his booty and go through the form of submission to Rome was offered a farm in Greece or Asia. By tens of thousands the pirates accepted these free land-grants, which made them better off than their honest and heavily taxed neighbours. Here was another proof, if one was needed, that piracy was a safe and profitable career. As soon as the Roman fleet was disbanded some of these new farmers went back to sea-roving; others joined Sextus Pompeius, the son of their conqueror, when thirty years later he set up as a pirate, during a later phase of the everlasting Roman civil war.

The Chieftain

But for the present the pirates were subdued. Pompeius was free to take over command of the army from Lucullus.

He did it ungraciously, for he was by nature ungracious. But the career of that great soldier and administrator, that politician more eager for titular honours than for power, that republican hero who could not brook an equal colleague, lies outside the scope of this book. He accorded Lucullus the bare minimum of ceremonial respect which was his due as a retired consul and Imperator, tried to spoil his Triumph by discharging all his soldiers before they reached Italy, and went out of his way to rescind every arrangement he had made for the government of Asia.

At last the Fimbrians went home as civilians. Lucullus kept as his ceremonial escort a mere 1,500 sick or wounded men, who were due for demobilization before the end of their full term of enlistment. The three other legions first brought oversea by Lucullus remained to swell the great army of Pompeius.

Nevertheless, Lucullus had his Triumph, for he had been a great conqueror. Since he had no army to march behind him the procession was short and meagre. But it included, besides the warlike trophies of mailed *cataphractarii*, scythed chariots, and the brazen beaks of 110 captured warships, an astonishing quantity of treasure. There was a life-sized statue of Mithradates made of gold, 20 litters piled with silver plate and 32 loaded with gold plate and decorated armour; 8 mules carried golden couches, 56 were laden with silver in bars and 107 with silver coin. All this was now the property of the Roman People, or of the gods in the Capitol. In addition every soldier received for himself 950 silver drachmae; and Lucullus remained one of the richest men in Rome.

Lucullus was remembered by posterity as a humane and honest governor of Asia. Yet even this honest Roman ruler took specie from the conquered east by the mule-load and the cart-load.

In the next generation Cicero, when governor of Cilicia, found desperate peasants in revolt against the tax-gatherers; Pliny, writing to the Emperor Trajan, laments that the cities of Asia are bankrupt and cannot pay for the public works which their councils, mindful of past glories, light-heartedly undertake. The money removed from the country by Lucullus, and later by Pompeius, was naked tribute, for which nothing was given in return.

Thus at the opening of the year 66 Pompeius lay in Cappadocia with a mighty host, while Mithradates held all inland Pontus with a small army of 30,000 foot and 3,000 horse. His realm was suffering from famine; for seven years the land of woods and mountains, which even in time of peace produced more timber than corn, had been ravaged by hostile armies. The devastation was most severe near the Cappadocian frontier; driven by hunger, Pontic outposts began to desert to the enemy. Mithradates did what he could to restore discipline, introducing the ghastly Roman punishment of crucifixion for captured deserters; but, whatever the punishment decreed by the King, his soldiers would not remain faithfully at their posts until they died of starvation.

If serious war came Mithradates must be beaten; and he knew it. But there was still ground for hope. Pompeius might not try very earnestly to conquer Pontus. The famous Roman soldier-politician was governed in all his actions by vanity and ambition; the centre of his world was Rome. As always, he knew that while he was absent in an unimportant corner of the world his enemies were making unpleasant speeches about him in the Forum. It was his particular misfortune that it was very easy to make Pompeius look a fool, and among the gifts showered upon him in his cradle his fairy godmother had omitted that of eloquence. If he had any political sense, and that was the only doubtful factor in the situation, he would be anxious to wind up the war as soon as possible and get home before he lost control of domestic politics.

Mithradates therefore opened tentative negotiations for peace. By now the utmost that he could ask for was confirmation of his rule in his hereditary dominions. If Pompeius would recognize him as client-King of Pontus he would be a faithful ally and friend of the Roman People; he would even send his contingent to the expected war against Armenia. His envoys added, unofficially, that the King still possessed a great hoard of gold and silver, and that Roman statesmen who spoke for peace would not go unrewarded.

But Pompeius was enjoying himself in the east, and with his

usual lack of political judgement he thought his authority in
Rome was secure. He demanded unconditional surrender,
though he held out hope that if Mithradates threw himself on
Roman mercy he might yet end his days a crowned King.
There was a bare chance that the negotiations might lead to a
dictated but not intolerable peace, when Pompeius laid down
one condition which Mithradates refused to accept. As a
guarantee of good faith, before anything else had been decided,
the King must surrender to the Roman army all the Roman
deserters in his camp.

Mithradates refused point-blank, though he knew that his
refusal meant a war which he could win only by a miracle.
Roman historians explain that the renegades were now the
most efficient part of the Pontic army, and that Mithradates
could no longer control them; if he had wished to hand them
over to ignominious execution they would have arrested him
first, before he could arrest them. It may be so, although native
Pontic volunteers made up most of the small army which still
served him. But the King had shown in the past that he was
skilful in plotting and intrigue; Pompeius and Mithradates
between them could have trapped the Popular exiles. It seems
just as likely that the King refused from a genuine scruple of
honour. He would not punish slaves or freedmen who followed
their lords into treason, because a vassal's loyalty to his lord
was the virtue he admired above all others. He expected his
own vassals to serve him faithfully, and, after all these years, the
Popular exiles might be considered his vassals. He would not
betray his own followers to their foes.

Negotiations were at an end. In his sixty-sixth year, bearing
the scars of three recent and serious wounds, the old King prepared for the hopeless struggle. Perhaps the Romans were sure
to overcome 33,000 starving men; and this was the very last
army of Pontus, with no reinforcements to be found anywhere.
But in war it is always too soon to admit defeat. He would keep
on trying, and give Pompeius as much trouble as he could.

The campaign opened with a cavalry skirmish; and it was a
sad portent of the times that the Romans were victorious. For
so long had the cavaliers of Pontus been supreme on the battlefield that they had grown too bold; they fell into a Roman
ambush. The Roman horse, presumably Galatians, pursued as

far as the main Pontic camp; in fact they very nearly overran the palisade, which would have dispersed the entire Pontic army. Just in time Mithradates himself led out the infantry. Since the legions were not yet on the field the Roman cavalry withdrew.

With his inferior force Mithradates dared not hazard a pitched battle in the open. As Pompeius advanced he must retire before him. He was desperately short of supplies, for he was operating in a famine-stricken country. But he hoped that as the Romans advanced behind him Pompeius in his turn would have difficulty in feeding his men.

It was a vain hope. On the battlefield Pompeius was a sound tactician of orthodox Roman principles; his greatness was displayed rather in the field of administration. His troops followed him willingly, because he always looked after their pay and supplies. Now, as he crossed from starving Cappadocia into starving Pontus, a well-organized baggage-train accompanied his army.

Mithradates had little room for manœuvre. If he retired before the Roman advance, waiting for a lucky opening, he would soon be driven up against the frontier of Armenia. Perhaps he had hoped, in the spring, that Tigranes would come to his assistance; now he knew that his son-in-law thought only of preserving the independence of his own Kingdom, and would never again, unless he was cornered, cross swords with a Roman army. Even if he dared not fight, Mithradates must soon make a stand. The Pontic army had now been under the guidance of Roman exiles for more than twenty years, and in his extremity the King adopted a device common in Roman tactics. He fortified a very strong camp on the summit of a lofty mountain, and tried to halt the advance of the invader by extensive trench-warfare.

That kind of operation demanded more discipline in daily camp-life, without the stimulus of daily fighting with the enemy, than could be expected from an army of enthusiastic but half-trained Asiatic mountaineers. The position chosen for Mithradates by his Roman advisers was certainly impregnable, but it was not easy to live in. Lack of water presently compelled him to withdraw. He had the mortification of seeing Pompeius comfortably installed in the strong lines he had built, where the disciplined legionaries dug wells to tap underground springs and obediently drank no more than their daily ration.

After another short retreat Mithradates once more entrenched his men to stand on the defensive. This time his camp was well supplied with food and water, and though not so strong as the last position still strong enough to make an assault a hazardous enterprise. Pompeius reconnoitred it, felt nervous, and decided that blockade would serve him better than battle.

From the Roman camp, pitched opposite, the invaders gradually extended their lines. Their trenches crept out on each flank, then curved forward; until at last they met again in rear of the Pontic army. Pompeius, enjoying a secure line of supply which stretched down to the Ionian coast, waited until hunger should compel the King to surrender.

The defenders endured an investment of forty-five days, and it is worthy of note that during this trial their discipline held firm. When food ran short they killed and ate their baggage-animals; but the King had given orders that the horses of the cavalry must be preserved at all costs, and the hungry soldiers obeyed.

At last the time came when they must break out, or surrender. For lack of transport the baggage must be left behind, and so must the sick. Every man unable to keep up with the march was killed by his comrades; which seems a ruthless massacre until we consider what would have been their fate as prisoners in Roman hands. In the middle of a dark night the Pontic cavalry broke through a weak spot in the line of investment, and the whole army followed.

Pompeius was quick to organize pursuit, and during the next day he caught up with the Pontic rearguard. The Roman exiles who surrounded the King were weary of endless retreating; perhaps, having lost all hope of victory, they wished to die fighting rather than by the sword of the executioner. They urged Mithradates to turn about and fall on the Roman van. But the King was determined to protract the war as long as possible; why die gallantly when tomorrow a change of government in Italy might bring about the recall of Pompeius and all his army? He used his splendid little handful of horse to drive in the front of the Roman column, then broke off the action and retired to another impregnable camp in the mountains.

The Chieftain

But this must be the end of the long retreat. Mithradates had been driven from end to end of the Kingdom of his ancestors. Behind his new position ran the river Euphrates, with on its farther shore the hostile, or at best neutral, Kingdom of Armenia. Perhaps it was as a symbolic reminder to his men, reminding them that now they must fight where they stood, that the site of the new camp, the ultimate camp, was a rocky peninsula bounded on three sides by the gorge of the river. Only one way led down from the crest of this ridge, and across this only path Pompeius soon lay encamped.

At last the Romans had cornered their elusive enemy, and they were eager to end the long campaign. On the very first day of the new siege skirmishing broke out at the advanced posts, skirmishing which gradually involved both armies. We are told that Mithradates had stationed four cohorts to defend the only path into his position. That is significant, as showing that by this time the Pontic foot had completely adopted Roman tactical formations. The Roman pickets advanced against these men. It was not a set assault, but a limited action intended to capture the little knoll occupied by the Pontic advanced post.

Presently the Pontic infantry began to be hard pressed, though they were not dislodged from their position. Late in the afternoon their commander sent a message back to headquarters, asking for reinforcements. Since there was no room for large numbers of men to engage on the narrow peninsula Mithradates did not put his whole force under arms. Only a few troops were needed, and he decided to send out his best troops, his cavalry; but because they were to hold broken ground they were marched off to fight dismounted.

When the Roman commander saw the defenders reinforced he of course in his turn called for more support. Pompeius sent forward his Galatian cavalry. Since they were attacking they came up on their horses; they tried to ride into the Pontic entrenchments while the dismounted Pontic troopers shot at them with arrows.

The reinforced Pontic line held firm, until presently the pressure of the attack slackened. At sunset the affair seemed to be going so well that the old King retired to his tent and went to bed. His sleep was disturbed by a vivid nightmare of shipwreck, and he started up with a cry that all was lost. Standing over his bed he saw frightened attendants who clamoured that all was indeed lost. The Romans were within the camp. Without an instant's delay the King must ride for his life.

The disaster had come about as the result of an absurd chapter of accidents. As the light failed the Galatian horse ceased their fruitless charges and prepared to retire to the Roman camp. The dismounted Pontic troopers, who had been fighting on the defensive all afternoon, saw an opportunity to deliver a telling blow on the retreating foe. But of course they would not attack dismounted. Without their horses cavalry are never very amenable to discipline; they think they have done their commander such a great favour by consenting to fight on foot that they deserve to conduct the battle as they see fit. The excited horsemen ran back pell-mell to their lines, eager to get into the saddle and cover themselves with glory.

In the dusk the Pontic infantry standing guard at the inner gate of the camp saw only a crowd of their own dismounted cavalry, running as fast as they could in no particular formation. They assumed that the outwork had been overrun, and that the Romans must be on the heels of their fleeing comrades. They fled from the gate, looking for a way of escape.

Suddenly the Galatian horse realized that the outwork had been evacuated. They advanced to occupy it, and sent back an urgent message to Pompeius. It was already nightfall, and at first Pompeius refused to commit his legions to a confused battle in the dark. Orders had already been issued for an assault in form on the next morning, and the only fault of Pompeius as a general was a certain reluctance to reshape in a hurry plans he had laid at leisure. But a deputation of centurions crowded into his tent, to remind him that the moon would rise almost immediately, and that it would rise behind the Romans; they would fight with the light at their backs, which was recognized to be a valuable tactical advantage. Furthermore, reports were coming in that the Pontic camp was in great confusion. Pompeius gave his permission, and the legions formed up for attack.

As they reached the hostile palisade the moon rose behind them. Staring into its light those Pontic archers who still stood to their posts could not make out the range, and shot off their arrows too soon. The Romans surged over the fortification,

They advanced slowly through the lines, delayed by the darkness and by their search for plunder. By the time his attendants woke Mithradates, organized Pontic resistance had collapsed.

The elderly King had never acquired the habit of sleeping alone. For this evening his companion was a Greek concubine named Hypsicratia. As he dressed in haste she also put on the armour of a Pontic guardsman, and took up sword and bow. Eight hundred horsemen of the bodyguard had collected round the bedchamber of their lord, and at their head the King charged the Roman line. It was impossible to break out by the only path, where the legions were densely massed; Mithradates, still in his sixty-seventh year the most dashing horseman in Asia, somehow got his horse down the cliff. But his guardsmen could not negotiate the steep descent. When dawn broke the King was riding north with only three companions; one of them was the sturdy Hypsicratia, a most useful concubine to take on an arduous campaign. In recognition of her gallantry Mithradates later issued a formal order that she was to be known in future by the masculine version of her name, Hypsicrates.

Out of 30,000 men in the Pontic army the Romans during the sack of the camp killed 10,000; and the remainder were dispersed in flight. But among those who escaped were stubborn patriots determined to continue the struggle against the invader; by the time Mithradates reached the remote fortress of Sinora, where he had a great treasure stored up against a rainy day, he was at the head of 3,000 infantry and a few squadrons of horse.

At Sinora, which lay on the frontier of Armenia, the King halted for a while. More stragglers joined him, but his army was still too weak to continue the war against the Romans. However, there were numerous castles under his command, and these castles held great treasures. He was as strong as he had been five years ago, when in 71 he first fled to Armenia. Once more he sent messages to his son-in-law, and perhaps himself ventured a short way into the neighbouring Kingdom.

Tigranes had made up his mind. The Romans were too strong to be withstood, and only by ruling as their faithful ally could he hope to keep his throne. He answered the appeal of Mithradates by putting a price of a thousand talents on the head of his fugitive father-in-law. There was no refuge in Armenia for the remnants of the Pontic army, or for the Roman exiles who still clung to their defeated protector.

Although it was now late in the year Mithradates could not remain where he was, for the Romans were marching on Sinora. He decided on an amazingly bold manœuvre. Since Armenia was barred to him he would march overland right round the eastern shore of the Euxine, picking up more troops in friendly Colchis and fighting his way through the land of the barbarous Achaeans. If all went well he must in the end come out on the eastern frontier of his own Kingdom of Bosporus, at present ruled by his unfaithful son Machares. It would be as much a journey of exploration as an operation of war, for no traveller had ever before traversed the whole of that route. The indomitable courage of the veteran of 66 is remarkable; it is even more remarkable that his men were willing to follow him, to give up all hope of seeing again their homes and families, to fight a way through savage and unknown lands to a remote, barbarous refuge.

Mithradates planned to start at once, and to pass the winter somewhere beyond the reach of Pompeius. But of course he had no transport, and he could not bear to abandon the bulky treasure stored in Sinora. He therefore divided among his men all the money he possessed, giving to each soldier a whole year's pay in advance, and making rich presents to his senior officers.

He must have been astonishingly certain of the fidelity of his men. They were about to leave their homes for ever, to undertake a hazardous march through unknown country; if all went well, this would bring them into lifelong exile. Yet Mithradates controlled only the ground on which his small force was encamped. The Armenian frontier lay close at hand, and Tigranes had already shown his hostility; the soldiers had all the world before them, and a year's pay in their wallets. Mithradates had guessed rightly; not one of his men deserted him. A chieftain who could inspire such devotion in a defeated army was more than the cruel and arbitrary tyrant who is put before us in histories written to please his Roman conquerors.

The great treasure, distributed among so many hands, could be carried easily. Mithradates set out for Colchis, the first stage on his dangerous journey. As soon as he left Pontus he had to fight his way through the levies of Iberia and Chotene, a small region tributary to Armenia. The Iberians, ancestors of the modern Georgians, did not oppose him very earnestly; they skirmished with arrows and javelins, but would not charge to close quarters. They must have known that this was not an expedition of conquest, to be resisted to the last man; for in later days they proved themselves a warlike people, very hard to subdue. When they had learned that they could not easily massacre the little army and steal its treasure they permitted it to pass through their country.

After he had won through this barrier Mithradates found himself in Colchis, where he was well received by men who had a few years ago been his obedient subjects. The town of Colchis was a flourishing port, and therefore accessible to Roman warships. For safety he went on a little farther, though he did not leave the land of Colchis. In a small place named Dioscurias he settled down with his men to pass the winter.

After Pompeius had pursued his fleeing enemy as far as the border of Lesser Armenia he turned back to complete the occupation of all the castles of Pontus. Many of these castles had been handed over as endowments to the discarded mistresses of Mithradates, and these women were naturally quite willing to desert the setting sun. Obeying the conventions of oriental politeness, they offered to enter the harem of their conqueror. But Pompeius, though as a young man he had been famous throughout Rome for his ardour in love, in the east chose to play the part of the incorruptible avenger of wrongs. He restored the ladies untouched to their parents; the more willingly, according to Plutarch, because 'the greater part were the daughters and wives of generals and princes'. This is the first we have heard of Mithradates as a wrecker of happy homes, and it should be noted that every one of his concubines who is mentioned by name was in origin a Greek courtesan. It seems more probable that Plutarch was misled by malicious gossip than that the King strained the loyalty of his senior officers by seducing their wives. He was nearer 70 than 60, a time of life when most rulers can resist the temptation to cuckold their most eminent subjects.

Mithradates had wronged no man when he took into his bed

Stratonice the harp-player. She was unmarried, and her father was a wandering minstrel, whose sudden wealth, the reward of his daughter's shame, nearly turned his head. The affair had begun in the brave days of 87, when Mithradates, in his vigorous forties, ruled Asia and Attica from his capital at Pergamum. Since then Stratonice had lived for many years in retirement; but since the King trusted her with his most valuable hoard of treasure he must have supposed he had given her no ground for discontent. Her residence was the hill-castle of Caenum; which housed not only a great sum of money, hidden underground in brazen casks, but also the confidential archives of the Kingdom of Pontus.

But Stratonice was ambitious for the future of the son she had borne to her master. As the offspring of a lowly concubine Xiphares was outside the customary line of succession, but there was a chance that the Roman conquerors would be looking for an obedient client-King. His devoted mother therefore sent out the loyal garrison of Caenum on a useless foray, and in their absence opened negotiations with Pompeius. If the Roman leader would promise to show favour to her son, and also permit her to keep her personal property, she would deliver to him the castle with its treasure and its even more valuable archives.

Pompeius at once agreed to the bargain; all the more willingly because Xiphares was then somewhere in Bosporus, so that he need promise no more than to spare his life if presently he should fall into Roman hands. Everyone was satisfied. Stratonice not only went free. She was allowed to decide for herself what proportion of the treasure of Caenum should be counted as her private property. The Romans gained a large sum of money; and documents were published, purporting to be the private papers of Mithradates, in which the King was shown as discussing projects for the assassination of his most faithful allies and subjects. This early demonstration of political warfare probably carried more weight with the simple Romans than with Asiatics, long accustomed to the use of forgery as a weapon to pull down the great.

After he had received the submission of every Pontic fortress Pompeius settled down into winter quarters at Amisus, and busied himself with the reorganization of the conquered country.

The Chieftain

His enemies (he was now prominent enough in Roman politics to have earned a great many enemies) noted ironically that while Mithradates was at large with an army to follow him the war could not be considered at an end, and that Pompeius had rebuked Lucullus for committing exactly the same breach of Roman constitutional law, the permanent organization of conquered territory before the final conquest had been achieved. But Pompeius at the head of a victorious and well-paid army was too great to be bound by the Roman constitution.

VII

The King of Bosporus

In the spring of 65 Mithradates continued his journey round
the eastern shore of the Euxine. His men knew they would
receive no more wages until they had installed him as King
in Panticapaeum; he had no money, while they had each at
least a year's pay with which to make a new start. But they
followed him willingly to the invasion of the land of the savage
Achaeans.

The Achaeans were routed in a single battle, and the march
continued. Probably the savage mountaineers did not resist
with great determination once they understood that the exiled
Pontic army was on its way to Bosporus, and had not come to
conquer and possess their land. But the 'Scythian Gates', a pass
in the main range of Caucasus, was a dangerous obstacle which
hitherto no army had surmounted. Mithradates won through it
successfully, to the amazement and admiration of the neighbouring tribes. During this march the old man, in his sixty-
seventh year, showed himself as vigorous and energetic as ever
Hannibal had been at the crossing of the Alps.

Once through the Scythian Gates the army emerged into the
steppe bordering the Sea of Azov, the steppe inhabited by
nomad tribes who had for generations been in treaty relations
with the Greek cities of the Crimea. The Scythian chiefs welcomed the return of their old ally. He flattered their vanity by
offering them some of his numerous daughters in marriage, and
in return was given much-needed supplies and recruits for his
cavalry.

For twenty-five years Machares, the youngest of the three
sons of Mithradates and his sister-Queen Laodice, had ruled
undisturbed in Bosporus. He had begun as his father's loyal
viceroy; but in 70, when the Romans first conquered Pontus,

he had prudently sent an offer of his allegiance to Lucullus. For the last six years he had been the friend and ally of the Roman People, an obedient and inoffensive client-King. He had taken it for granted that his father had been finally eliminated from politics, and that so long as he paid tribute to the Romans he would rule peacefully in the remote Kingdom which had come to him by chance. Now suddenly the old man appeared out of the blue, having accomplished a march through unexplored territory which was supposed to be impossible for a regular army. The middle-aged despot was overcome by terror.

To begin with he sent envoys to excuse his conduct, explaining that only fear of the Romans had driven him to betray his family. Of course the excuse was absurd, as he knew very well. Lucullus had never menaced him, and his spontaneous offer of allegiance had taken the Romans by surprise. The envoys returned, to report that old Mithradates was indeed very angry with his treacherous son. In fear of his life, Machares fled over Straits of Kertch to the Crimea.

Such was his terror that he burned every ship he could not take with him, to hamper pursuit. But against an army which had marched overland from Pontus to Bosporus such precautions were vain; the old King soon gathered other shipping, and made ready for an attack on Panticapaeum. Seeing himself cornered, Machares swallowed a fatal dose of the traditional Pontic poison.

When Mithradates had finally crossed the straits and completed his great journey he was unchallenged sovereign of all Bosporus. He put to death every one of his own servants and henchmen who had worked for his usurping son. But for those who had from the beginning been servants of Machares, not of Mithradates, there was mercy and confirmation in office; for it was the fixed foundation of the old King's policy that a vassal could do no wrong so long as he obeyed his lord. The only innocent sufferer was Xiphares, who was killed by his father to vex his mother. To add to the anguish of the unfaithful Stratonice her son's body was left unburied; and therefore, according to the popular belief of the Greeks, his spirit would never find rest.

In the autumn, about the time of his sixty-seventh birthday, for the first time in his life the old warrior was disabled by sickness. The most tiresome symptoms were ulcers on the face, caused perhaps by the strange food he had eaten during his terrible journey over Caucasus. As much because he was ashamed of his ravaged appearance as to spare his strength he shut himself up in his private apartments to be nursed by his eunuchs, while the same eunuchs ruled the country without supervision from their master. But he did not relinquish all control of affairs. He sent envoys to Pompeius, offering to recognize the Romans as rulers of Pontus if they in their turn would recognize him as independent King of Bosporus; and, expecting that his proposals for peace would be rejected, he ordered his eunuch ministers to raise as large an army as the resources of his diminished Kingdom would permit.

In the spring of the same year, 65, Pompeius set out in pursuit of the fugitive King; though he can hardly have expected to catch up with him, for by passing the winter in arranging the affairs of Pontus he had allowed Mithradates a start of at least four months. But Pompeius was thinking more of the renown he would gain in Rome by leading his army beyond the limits of the known world than of avenging the massacre of 88. The people of Colchis submitted as soon as he invaded their land, and he learned from them that his veteran antagonist had vanished into the unknown and impassable mountains of the north. He easily persuaded himself that no more would be heard of Mithradates; who ought to be killed, at his age, by the hardships of the journey. It would be more profitable, he thought, and more glorious, to march to the Caspian, to which the Roman Eagles had never before penetrated, than to pursue a worn-out old man through barren mountain passes; it would give his supporters in Rome something to boast about. Before he reached the main range of Caucasus he turned eastward and headed for the inland sea.

It has been suggested that this change of plan was inspired by far-sighted economic considerations. Pompeius is said to have been worried at the interruption of trade with the Far East, now that hostile Parthians blocked the terminus of the old trade route from China to Mesopotamia; perhaps he planned to open a new route from the Caspian. But Roman generals were not usually interested in economic planning. It is more likely that the love of adventure led him on.

His new move brought him into collision with the Albanians and Iberians, fierce mountaineers who assembled to dispute his passage. A great host of 70,000 men tried to ambush him on the edge of a tangled forest. The Romans stood firm and drove the barbarians back into the woods. They then surrounded the forest and set it ablaze (which suggests that the season must have been high summer; though Plutarch, confused in his account of this campaign, tells of a barbarian night-attack which in vain hoped to take advantage of the normal Roman drunkenness at Saturnalia, in December). Many of the savages were killed, and the rest offered submission to Rome.

Among the dead on the battlefield, and among the hostages delivered when the enemy sought peace, were armed women. Their local guides explained to the Romans that among the tribes of Caucasus women as well as men turned out to repel invasion. But Pompeius, snatching at a plausible excuse to add to the fame of his exploits, reported to Rome that he had conquered the fabled land of the Amazons. To prove it he reserved some of these hostages for display in his future Triumph.

The Albanians submitted all the more readily because the Romans at once moved on from their territory, advancing towards the Caspian. Of course as soon as they had seen the backs of the invading army the new subjects of Rome withdrew their submission. Pompeius seized on this excuse to return. He had reached the Caspian at a point where its shore was an uninviting desert, and his men complained that the multitude of poisonous snakes made it dangerous to bivouac in the open. Enough had been done for glory. Pompeius marched once more through the land of the Albanians, defeated them for a second time, and came back to the shore of the Euxine in Colchis.

He traversed a waterless stretch of his return journey by making his men carry 10,000 skins filled with water. There lay the real strength of the Roman army, as much as in the broadswords of the legionaries. In their place Asiatics would have marched with empty water-skins, to save themselves a heavy burden; or if they could have been persuaded to carry water they would have drunk it all at the first halt.

In Colchis there was still no news of Mithradates. To be on

the safe side Pompeius ordered his fleet to watch the ports of the Chersonese, and be ready to fight if the King sent ships to win back the Greek cities on the Pontic coast. The warships of the first century could not maintain a close blockade unless they had a friendly base very near at hand, since they could not keep the open sea for more than a few days without putting into harbour to rest the rowers; but fast cruisers could look into Panticapaeum and then report back to Sinope. Soon it was accepted that Rome controlled the Euxine; not even merchant ships from Asia could reach Bosporus.

It is possible that Pompeius was planning a Roman invasion of Bosporus by sea, when he was distracted by the offer of another and easier conquest. The Crown Prince of Armenia, in rebellion against his father, sought the help of the Romans in a war against his own country. Here was a chance to surpass the greatest achievement of Lucullus; who had indeed penetrated to Artaxata, but had been forced by mutiny to retire, leaving the fortress untaken. Until these laurels had been harvested Mithradates could wait. In early autumn Pompeius led the great Roman army south-eastwards from Colchis to the invasion of Armenia.

The unfilial and disloyal Crown Prince was another Tigranes, the third and only surviving son of King Tigranes and Queen Cleopatra, daughter of King Mithradates. Of his two elder brothers one had been killed in battle while leading a rebel army against his father, the second had been executed for treason because, when he saw the King take a bad fall in the hunting-field, he had galloped off to seize the throne instead of waiting to see if the old man would get up again. On that occasion young Tigranes had stayed by his father and helped him to rise; later, riding in the rout after the battle of Tigranocerta, he had refused the diadem which his father pressed on him. He had earned the reputation of a loyal and dutiful son. But the ruling house of Armenia followed the normal custom of a Hellenistic royal family; when he saw an invincible army of foreigners poised on the frontier, young Tigranes snatched at this excellent opportunity to seize the crown before it should descend to him in the ordinary course of nature.

The alliance of young Tigranes was all the more valuable to Pompeius because the prince, after the failure of his initial revolt, had fled to the Parthian court. There he had married the daughter of the King of the Parthians; when he submitted to Rome it might be assumed that he brought with him the friendship of Parthia.

Pompeius marched unopposed into the heart of Armenia. He was delighted to find that even the royal fortress of Artaxata, which had defied Lucullus, was now ready to open its gates and receive a Roman garrison. Old King Tigranes had heard a good deal about the character of the enemy leader, and he had decided that in his desperate situation flattery would be more fruitful than an effort to fight to the last. While the Romans lay encamped outside the undefended capital they heard that the King was approaching, eager to beg mercy from his conqueror. Of set purpose Roman pride made the interview as humiliating as possible. Outside the camp King Tigranes was arrested by lictors, as though a petty criminal were being brought to judgement; he was compelled to dismount, for only friends of Rome might pass a Roman palisade on horseback. The King without hesitation did even more than had been asked. Before he entered on foot the presence of the great Imperator he spontaneously surrendered his sword; at the feet of Pompeius the unarmed man removed his diadem, and cast himself prostrate on the ground.

These tactics were completely successful. Pompeius raised the suppliant to his feet, embraced him, and then gratified his own vanity by sitting publicly on his tribunal between two Kings, father and son, while he divided their realm and ended a civil war.

Tigranes the elder made certain of Roman friendship by making Pompieus a present of 6,000 talents of silver, and distributing money throughout the army at the rate of fifty drachmae for each soldier, 1,000 for each centurion, and 10,000 for each military tribune. It was easily agreed that the King might keep his ancestral realm, Armenia proper, provided that all his conquests in Syria should pass into Roman hands. Tigranes the younger was confirmed as heir to his father, and in the interim compensated with the petty Kingdom of Sophene. Thus Pompeius did not in fact raise the power of Rome any higher than it had stood when Lucullus was called home against his will; but Lucullus had never seen a great King prostrate before him,

or been asked to divide a Kingdom. Pompeius preened himself
with pride, and so long as he held power in Rome the independence of Armenia was safe.

King Tigranes, naturally, was as pleased as Pompeius. Except
for the slight on his dignity, he was as well off as if he had
repelled a dangerous invasion by force of arms; even his purse
had not been drained to the bottom, for it must have worked
out cheaper to buy off the Romans than to fight them. The only
dissatisfied member of the peace conference was the Crown
Prince, who had expected something better than the puny
realm of Sophene. In addition he was annoyed to see his father
dissipate the royal treasure which he might expect one day to
come to himself. Foolishly young Tigranes insulted the great
Imperator, and was suspected of plotting another revolt against
his father. Pompeius suddenly recalled that, although he could
not catch Mithradates, he had in his power a grandson of his
great antagonist, who would make a most impressive ornament
for his Triumph. The prince was arrested, kept in chains at
Roman headquarters, and in 62 taken to Italy, despite the pro-
tests of his father-in-law the King of the Parthians. He figured
in the splendid Triumph of Pompeius, a Triumph which
brought into the Roman treasury 20,000 talents, plunder which
had been the working capital of the international merchants of
Asia, plunder which completed the financial ruin of the unfortunate peninsula. Whn the procession had arrived at the
Capitol, and there was no further use for living trophies, young
Tigranes was strangled; for such was the ancient custom of
Rome. He had shown a spark of his grandfather's spirit, but
without any trace of his grandfather's patience and wisdom.

While the Romans lay outside Artaxata the envoys from
Bosporus reached Pompeius with their offer of peace. Pompeius
returned the curt answer that there could be no peace until
Mithradates should kneel before him to beg mercy, as Tigranes
had knelt. It seems likely that if the old King had yielded mercy
would have been granted to him, for Pompeius was proud of
his magnanimity. But Mithradates also had his pride, and there
were no further negotiations.

The Roman soldiers took it for granted that their next task
would be the invasion of Bosporus. Though they had already
discovered that they could not follow the famous overland

retreat of their great enemy, their fleet was supreme in the Euxine, and there was nothing to stop a sea-borne invasion. But Pompeius had lost interest in such remote lands; or rather, his imagination had been inflamed by the fabled splendours of Syria. First he tidied up the situation in Asia; poor old Ariobarzanes was restored to a greater Cappadocia, Deiotarus was rewarded with a greater Galatia, cities were founded to commemorate the final expulsion of Mithradates at Nicopolis, and also, oddly enough, to commemorate the Roman defeat at Zela; then Pompeius led his army south, to Jerusalem and on to Arabia; and so disappeared from the theatre of operations.

Meanwhile in Bosporus the indomitable old King was planning to continue the war. In his sixty-eighth year he was still a mighty warrior, a horseman capable of riding 120 miles in a single day. But in his old age the witty and luxurious feaster, the enlightened patron of Greek letters, had grown morose and solitary. To preserve his health he had abandoned the pleasures of the table, though the pleasures of the alcove still consoled him. He shut himself up in his seraglio, where he saw no one but his women and the eunuchs who governed them. From time to time his ministers reported to him; and always they received the same instructions, that the whole resources of his Kingdom must be devoted to the coming war.

In his solitary mind a stupendous fantasy had taken shape. He knew the east, and he knew that in the east the Romans were too strong to be overthrown; even the Euxine, just outside the harbour of his capital of Panticapaeum, was controlled by the Roman fleet, and in a Kingdom based on the treeless steppe he could not build ships to defeat it. He had been told that in the unknown west the frontiers of Rome were less secure. The Roman exiles who still followed his fallen fortunes would remind him that recently a great host of Germans had come southward over the Alps; no Roman ever forgot that long ago a Gallic horde had sacked Rome herself. It would seem in the memory of an old man only yesterday that the Italian cities were leagued against their mistress, and even more recently Sertorius his friend and ally had ruled supreme in Spain. In the west the Populars had been strong and successful; in the west great armies of Romans had been annihilated.

The King of Bosporus

On the map, or what passed for a map in the first century, it looked quite easy. Just to the west of his Kingdom lay the mouths of the Danube. If you marched up the whole length of the great river you would arrive north of the Alps, without any danger of losing your way; when you had crossed the mountains by the gentle Brenner Pass you would be among the war-like tribes of Cisalpine Gaul and the wealthy but oppressed cities of Etruria, all stout and recently defeated enemies of Rome. Surely a leader who could bring his men overland from Colchis to Bosporus would find no difficulty in marching up a broad and level river-valley? It so happened that he was already known to many of the barbarian tribes on this route; he had encouraged the Thracians to attack Roman Macedonia, and he had hired mercenaries from the easterly Gauls of the upper Danube.

That was it. He would march from the Euxine to the Alps, gathering barbarian allies as he marched. He would conquer Italy from the north, while the main Roman army hunted him in the east. He would end his days as King of the known world, a greater King even than Alexander or Darius.

Because the project was very difficult, and because in fact it failed, we are inclined to dismiss it as absurd. The Romans, who knew their own world, were genuinely afraid of it. It is a fact attested by archaeology that the iron-age dwellers in Austria and Bohemia derived much of their culture from the metal-workers of the steppe. The Ostrogoths took a long time to ride from the Ukraine to Italy, but they rode there in the end; the Huns and the Mongols rode from central Asia to Germany; Hannibal took his infantry overland from Cartagena in Spain to Calabria. A nucleus of trained soldiers, with enough money to pay their way, could march a very long way among friendly barbarians, who were usually glad to welcome strangers provided the strangers did not intend to stay permanently in their land.

But at long last Mithradates was running short of money; perhaps the treason of Stratonice had deprived him of his last, most essential, war-reserve. His plan of campaign called for a small force of well-trained veteran troops. His savage allies would fill the ranks with whooping spearmen; but there must be smart guardsmen to impress the Gallic chieftains with his grandeur, and catapults, battering-rams, and siege towers such as Gauls had never seen. Unless he had these things he would be received on the upper Danube as a defeated fugitive, not as a dangerous foe of Rome.

It was easy to find recruits for the royal guard. Soon 36,000 men were embodied, divided into sixty cohorts each of 600 men. This was the exact equivalent of six Roman legions, divided tactically in exactly the same manner; they must have been trained and commanded by the Popular exiles at the Bosporan court.

But the pay and equipment of these troops cost money, and all the money had to be raised from the slender resources of Bosporus. Siege engines in particular were lavish consumers of scarce raw material. The Hellenistic catapult was tactically an anti-personnel weapon rather than a machine for battering stone walls, as is shown by its name, catapeltes=shield-piercer. It propelled a heavy barbed javelin by the sudden release of twisted ropes; and these ropes must be made of some elastic material. The only elastic fibres known to the ancients, who had no rubber, were the long hair of women and the sinews of oxen. The larger engines must be built with massive timber, which on the steppe was scarce and valuable. Mithradates, nursing his ulcered face in the privacy of the harem, left practical details to his ministers, the eunuchs who attended him. These eunuchs displayed the indifference to the welfare of ordinary mankind which seems to be normal in that species.

They scoured the land for timber, felling big trees without compensating their owners. They cut off the hair of free-born women without first asking the consent of their husbands. They seized the indispensable plough-oxen in the fields, to butcher them for their sinews; though it meant that the peasants would have no harvest in the autumn. They took all the wealth of the prosperous, and the savings of the humble.

In fact they behaved as officials behave nowadays. If we should suffer the same oppression we should merely shrug our shoulders and remind one another that there was a war on. But the eunuchs of Mithradates were dealing with the subjects of an ancient oriental despotism, not with the citizens of a modern western democracy. The backward people of Bosporus had never been taught that a government at war has an absolute right to everything of value in the country it governs.

The King of Bosporus

Phanagoria, on the eastern mainland opposite Panticapaeum, was the first city to rise in revolt. After one of the King's eunuch ministers had been murdered in the street the citizens flocked together in arms. The citadel held out for Mithradates, since he had made it a receptacle for minor and unwanted members of the royal family. It held three of his young sons and a daughter, under the guardianship of their grown-up brother Artaphernes, a man in his forties. Elsewhere in the town was the dwelling of another of the King's daughters, Cleopatra, who seems to have been of full age. Of course all these lesser children were the offspring of concubines, not of royal Queens. In normal times they would not have been considered important; but Mithradates had now no legitimate son to succeed him, and as yet he had not nominated his successor.

The guards in the citadel resisted until the building began to burn. Then they surrendered, and the children of Mithradates became prisoners of the rebellious mob. Cleopatra, whose house must have been by the water-side, maintained a stout defence until ships of the royal navy rescued her and carried her over the straits to the Crimea.

Except for Panticapaeum, the capital, all the towns of Bosporus joined in the revolt. But the army, encamped round the King's palace, remained loyal. Mithradates at last emerged from his seclusion to negotiate with the rebel leaders. The result of these negotiations cannot be accurately ascertained; but it seems that a vague and ill-defined peace was patched up, after the manner of the agreed *communiqué* issued at the end of a modern international conference, which bears a different meaning for each signatory. Preparations for war were now completed, so taxation could be lightened; the King got back his children, and a few ringleaders were punished. The Greek cities of Bosporus still acknowledged Mithradates as King, but they were free to manage their own internal affairs. It was taken for granted that next year, when he set out on his great expedition, he would leave them with full self-government.

In the autumn of 64 Mithradates celebrated his sixty-eighth birthday. He still took his daily dose of 'the antidote', followed by a little poison to prove that the drug was working properly; as the result of, or in spite of, this régime he continued to enjoy excellent physical health. He was fully competent to command an army in the field; he could ride his 120 miles in a day, and throw a javelin as well as any of his soldiers. He was surrounded by a numerous harem, which produced an annual crop of royal children. His bodily vigour was the marvel of all who knew him.

He was worried about what would happen to these children after he had set off on his great march. In particular he could not take his daughters with him; yet if anyone blemished their chastity the insult would reflect on the King their father. The obvious solution was to marry them off as quickly as possible, and so transfer the keeping of their honour to their husbands. He despatched all those who were old enough to travel as wives for the Scythian chiefs who had befriended him when he emerged from his famous crossing of Caucasus. The soldiers who escorted the girls could at the same time ask the Scythians to send him more recruits for his great army of invasion.

But now, in the winter of 64, the arm of the King's vengeance had shrunk to a very short compass. In his presence his soldiers still obeyed the stern old man, so brave, so wise, so strong, so terrifying. When they were out on the open steppe they could see that he was no more than a defeated rebel, making defiant faces in a corner because the Romans had not bothered to pursue him. The soldiers found themselves commanded by the unpopular court eunuchs, and they knew that what they guarded was of great value. They murdered their eunuch commanders, and then took the virgins to the nearest Roman garrison.

The King could do nothing to punish their treachery. He ruled no more than the ground on which his small army was encamped. But that army still obeyed him, and he was determined to make one more attack on the Romans while he still had the strength to ride a horse. As the spring of 63 melted the frost of the steppe the long march up the valley of the Danube loomed nearer. It seemed to his men every day more hazardous. What could cheerfully be planned over the wine-cups of a winter feast was much less inviting when the grass began to grow and the baggage animals were ready. Still Mithradates betrayed no hesitation. Men whispered that he did not hope for success; he would march against Italy because he knew his end was near and he was determined to die in harness.

The King of Bosporus

Every soldier in the army was apprehensive; but the most frightened were the Roman exiles. Rather than live under an Optimate government they had fled to the ends of the earth. If ever they had possessed the courage to attack the Capitol they would not have begun by running away to the far side of the Euxine; it would have been simpler to stay in Italy and fight for the Popular cause. They had thought themselves safe as suppliants at the court of a King so far away, and now he talked of leading them back to the lion's den! But they were Romans, surrounded by barbarians. Pride kept them from open mutiny, even while they looked round for an excuse to abandon the hare-brained project.

In this state of affairs a son of the King named Pharnaces saw his chance of seizing the throne. He was about 35 years of age, the son of a concubine and therefore not a royal prince; but he was more energetic and competent than any of his numerous half-brothers, and the old King talked of making him his heir. Yet what heritage would be left for the successor of Mithradates unless he acted at once? Presently, when news should come to Bosporus that the puny royal army had been overwhelmed by the barbarians of the Danube, the cities of the little Kingdom would seek the protection of Rome. Unless the war was stopped the heir of Mithradates would find himself without subjects to govern. Pharnaces began to plot the overthrow of his father.

The conspiracy was betrayed, and the conspirators bloodily punished. But Menophanes, a trusted Greek general who had served the King faithfully ever since he campaigned for him in Greece twenty-five years ago, persuaded him to show mercy to his misguided son. He pointed out that the execution of the heir would be an unlucky prologue for the start of the great expedition, and that by intriguing for a crown before it should come to him in the course of nature Pharnaces had done no more than display the spirit of his ancestors. Mithradates loved the only competent son left to him; in the end he was prevailed on, for the first time in his life, to pardon a traitor. The young man was not even imprisoned. He was reconciled with his father and allowed to go free, and it was agreed that when the army set out on its great march he should stay behind and govern Bosporus as viceroy.

Pharnaces did not trust his good fortune. He was convinced

that his father was only biding his time, and would have him
put out of the way later. As soon as he was released he went
straight to the quarters of the Roman exiles, and begged them
to join him in ending the hopeless war. The Romans already
shared his opinion; now they convinced themselves that to take
sides in an internal conflict was not the same thing as to desert
their host and protector. On the very evening of his release
Pharnaces won the support of these exiles; at once he sent
agents to approach the troops in the other camps outside
Panticapaeum.

Early the next morning Mithradates was awakened by the
sound of tumult in the nearby camps. When he sent messengers
to discover the cause he soon received the answer of the
mutineers. They announced shortly that they would no longer
be ruled by an old man who was himself ruled by his eunuchs,
an old man who had slain his children, his ministers and his
friends. Instead they would serve his son, a fine young King.

There had been no time for Pharnaces to make contact with
the whole army; but as news of the mutiny spread the whole
army joined in the revolt. Even the sailors of the fleet, whom no
one had bothered to inform, shouted for Pharnaces as soon as
they heard of the revolution.

Mithradates took the only course open to him. He put on his
armour, mounted a showy warhorse, and went out to parley
with the mutineers. The guards who held his palace were still
loyal to him; but as he came out on the parade ground the
soldiers at a neighbouring post began to shout for Pharnaces.
At once the King turned on these nearest traitors, hoping that
if here he made an example of their comrades might be recalled
to duty. The post was within arrow range of the palace, and the
loyal guards began to shoot at it.

The little blockhouse was not designed to withstand attack
from this inner side, and its garrison at once ran for the nearest
rebel camp. The rebels, safe behind their palisade, cried out
that these eleventh-hour recruits might not share the reward of
successful treason until they had demonstrated that they were
not merely joining the winning side, but actually helping it to
victory.

The group from the blockhouse took the hint, and turned to
attack Mithradates. The King was in his sixty-ninth year, he

had been suddenly called from his bed, and at that hour of the morning he was probably full of antidote and its accompanying dose of Pontic poison. But he had fought his way out of tight corners before, and he was still the best horseman in Asia. Charging his attackers, he cut his way clear through them, though as he won clear his horse was killed under him. On foot and alone the old man then fought his way back to his palace.

He climbed to a watch-tower on the highest point of the citadel. Below him he could see the soldiers he had trained, whose lavish equipment had cost him the loyalty of his subjects. Not one of them obeyed him now, save for the guards who held the palace.

There had been a time when he waged war against Rome at the head of the united forces of Greece and Asia; he had continued the struggle as leader only of the mountaineers of Pontus; he had been driven from the land of his ancestors, and then had returned in triumph; even in this remote corner of the world he had recruited a dangerous army; for twenty-five years he had been the implacable enemy of Rome. Now he had come to the end of the road. He was no longer a King; he no longer led an army. For the first time since he embarked on his hazardous career he took thought for the preservation of his own life.

In utter despair he sent envoys to beg Pharnaces to permit him to go into exile, reminding him that only yesterday he himself had spared his rebellious son and set him at liberty. As soon as these envoys reached the lines of his enemy and successor they joined the winning side. He could hardly blame them; that was the accepted pattern of Hellenistic politics. Presently he saw the mutineers clustering together in the open. His treacherous son appeared, surrounded by senior officers. He was led to an improvised throne, and there crowned with a broad leaf in default of a diadem; since the remaining crown jewels, those which had not been sold to equip the army, were still lodged in the citadel.

That was final. A son who publicly seized his father's throne could not show mercy to his predecessor. If he yielded he would be handed over to the Romans, those experts in the infliction of degrading and cruel death. There was only one way of escape.

Two years ago, when at Sinora he distributed the last treasure of Pontus, he had hidden a lethal dose of Pontic poison in the hollow pommel of his sword. But even in his last hour he remained the chieftain, whose first care must be the welfare of his dependents. Out of all his numerous children two daughters remained in the citadel; and there were the loyal guards to be saved, if it could be done. He ordered the soldiers who still obeyed him to go out and offer their services to Pharnaces, for the King their master had no more need of armed men. But Pharnaces and the rebel army could not but fear Mithradates so long as he remained alive; when they saw soldiers issue from the palace they thought the old King must be leading a last desperate attack. Most of the loyal guardsmen were killed before they had time to explain that the war was ended.

The two girls had been reared as royal princesses, though their mothers must have been concubines; Mithradatis had been betrothed to the King of Egypt and Nysa to his brother the King of Cyprus. But now no King would marry them to gain the alliance of the mighty King of Pontus; if they were captured they would be reserved to walk as trophies in the Triumph of Pompeius, and then sold for what they would fetch in the slave-market of Rome. Their father advised them to beg mercy from Pharnaces, but they insisted on sharing his poison. Their lives had been sheltered, and they had never bothered with the antidote; they died quickly and painlessly.

The old King swallowed what was left in his sword-hilt. He walked rapidly about the room, to encourage the poison to flow through his veins. But more than fifty years of the daily antidote had immunized his body, and the drug failed to affect him. At last he understood that he could not die by poison. There was still in his following a Gallic nobleman, a chieftain of Galatia who stood by his lord to the last. Mithradates turned to Bituitus, reminding him that for many years he had relied on his sharp sword and strong right arm. 'But although I have been on my guard against all the poisons that a man may take with his food, I have neglected to provide against that most deadly poison, to be found in every royal palace: the treason of soldiers, of sons, and of friends.' Obeying orders to the last, Bituitus cut him down.

Next day Pharnaces despatched a trireme to Sinope. It carried the body of his father, the soldiers who had been responsible for the capture and execution of Manius Aquilius twenty-five years ago, and the few hostages whom Mithradates had still kept by him. The new King offered to serve the Romans as a loyal ally and friend if they would allow him to rule the Kingdom of Bosporus. The offer was accepted.

Pompeius was leading his army against the stronghold of Petra in Arabia when messengers, their spears wreathed in laurel as though to report a great victory, brought the news that his stubborn antagonist was dead. So eager was he to proclaim the glad tidings to his men that he could not wait until the customary tribunal had been built in the new camp; but jumped up on a heap of pack-saddles and at once made an extempore speech. His enemies had been complaining that he neglected his duty, which was to hunt down Mithradates, while he increased his fame by marching to regions which had never before been visited by a Roman army. Now he was free to use his cohorts in domestic politics. He immediately called off the campaign against the Arabs, and marched at full speed for Amisus.

When he reached the Euxine he inspected the corpse of his mighty adversary. Pharnaces, anxious above all to curry favour with the invaders of his country, had loaded the trireme with a splendid offering; besides the body of Mithradates and the bodies of his two daughters there were the royal robes and parade armour of the dead King. At first Pompeius suspected an attempt to deceive him; Mithradates was capable of spreading a report of his own death while he marched secretly up the Danube. When the coffin was opened he was still in doubt; for though Pharnaces had given orders that his father's body should be embalmed the undertakers were unskilful, and the face in particular had decayed. But further examination showed the Romans that this must be the genuine article. The trunk was intact; the trunk of a man nearly seventy years of age, a man still strong and vigorous, capable of riding 120 miles in a day or of fighting his way out of a group of mutineers, a man immune to disease or poison, so strong that he could only be killed by the edge of the sword, a man who in his late sixties could fight all day in the front rank, a man who had recently received, and recovered from, three serious wounds, a man of almost divine height, strength, and symmetry. Pompeius was convinced. In the whole of Roman history there had been only one man of that kind. He had before him the body of Mithradates Eupator, sixteenth in descent from Darius Hystaspes the Great King, eighth in descent from the first King of independent Pontus.

The conquerors marvelled at the armour which had been made for the dead King. Its size proved his more than human height and strength, but the costly workmanship was even more impressive. Pompeius of course reserved such a splendid trophy for his Triumph, but he was not always served with honesty. A Roman stole the magnificent baldric, said to be worth 400 talents of silver, to sell it to Ariarathes of Cappadocia; another Roman stole the diadem, and gave it as a present to Faustus, the worthless son of the great Sulla. There was so much peculation that if the King was to be buried decently Pompeius must defray the cost from his own purse.

Pompeius treated the remains of his famous adversary with reverence. He paid for a dignified burial in the royal mausoleum near Sinope, where lay the tombs of other members of the extinct dynasty.

Pharnaces was confirmed as client-King of Bosporus, save for the one city of Phanagoria. That was made a little Kingdom by itself, ruled by one Castor who had led the final revolt; for special honour must be paid to the city which had taken the initiative in the downfall of the dreaded Mithradates.

Epilogue

Pompeius returned to Rome, where for the next fifteen years he stood at the head of affairs. Naturally, the east also remained as he had ordered it. Presently Pharnaces recovered Phanagoria; then, ruling quietly in Bosporus, he gave no trouble to anyone.

No more is heard of the Roman exiles who had lived at his father's court. They must by now have been old men; either they settled down and their children became Bosporans, or they went home quietly, one by one.

In 49 the great Roman civil war flared up again. Pompeius, by this time the leader, or at least the ally, of the oligarchs, was driven from Italy by Julius Caesar at the head of the Populars. During the winter of 49–48 Pompeius held almost exactly the territory that had been held by Mithradates in 88, Greece and all Asia as far as the Euphrates. In a Roman civil war money was one of the most important weapons, and during the struggle the noble rulers of the east squeezed both the cities and the peasantry to the uttermost farthing. By the time that Pompeius met defeat, at Pharsalus in June 48, Roman rule was detested by all her eastern subjects. Pompeius fled by sea from Greece to Egypt, where he was murdered as he disembarked. The legions which normally formed the garrison of Asia had been killed or captured at Pharsalus; the propraetors and legates installed by the oligarchs had fled to continue the war in Africa. For a brief interval the east was without a regular administration.

King Pharnaces suddenly remembered that he was the son of the great Mithradates. On the spur of the moment, without diplomatic preparation, he sailed across the Euxine to invade Pontus, the land of his ancestors. He brought with him only his small standing army of Bosporan Greeks, and a few Scythian mercenaries. He had no money, and no siege engines.

At first the desperate gamble met with success. Sinope opened its gates, and the citizens of Amisus sent word that they would

come over to him as soon as he appeared with an army outside
their walls. As Pharnaces marched thither he encountered
Domitius Calvinus, an eminent soldier of the Popular faction
who had commanded Caesar's centre at Pharsalus. The scratch
Roman force was completely defeated; the heir of the ancient
Persian line ruled once more in Pontus.

During the winter Pharnaces intrigued with the chieftains of
Galatia, who saw the east without a master and were anxious to
keep on good terms with every neighbouring power. Caesar,
who had sailed in pursuit of Pompeius directly from Greece to
Egypt, soon heard of this threat to his overland communications. First he was detained in Alexandria by a pointless Egyptian dynastic squabble, then he squandered the early spring in
sightseeing on the upper Nile with the charming Queen Cleopatra. But by high summer he was marching north with 3,000
of his own veterans, and reinforcements collected from the
Roman garrisons in Syria. He paused at Tarsus to hold a con-
gress of local rulers, and there persuaded the Galatian chiefs
that Roman rule would soon return. On the 2nd of August 47
he encountered the Pontic army at Zela, the old battlefield on
which Mithradates had defeated Triarius in 67. The troops of
Pharnaces were so easily put to flight that Caesar could report
his success to the Senate, in three contemptuous words: *Veni,
vidi, vici*—I came, I saw, I conquered.

Of course Caesar was eager to diminish the fame of Pompeius,
his great antagonist. It was sound propaganda to describe the
men of Pontus as contemptible foes. But Caesar wrote under the
eyes of jealous enemies and rivals; he could not have dismissed
the battle in three words unless it had been in fact an easy
victory. That reflects the more honour on Mithradates, who
with the same material expelled the Romans from Asia, conquered much of Greece, and from first to last maintained the
struggle against a more powerful adversary for twenty-five years.

Pharnaces rallied the remnants of his army, for one of the
virtues of these Pontic soldiers was that they would come again
after a defeat. Caesar, anxious to get back to Rome, could not
spare time to crush him; he left the winding up of the campaign
to Domitius Calvinus. Pharnaces was allowed to retire unmolested from Sinope to Bosporus; but for lack of shipping he
was compelled to kill the horses of his Scythian cavalry.

Epilogue

Arrived in Bosporus he found of course that the citizens had revolted, under the leadership of a certain Asander. It was the normal custom for his subjects to desert a beaten King; which reminds us again of the achievement of Mithradates, who kept the loyalty of his followers through so many defeats. Undismayed, Pharnaces made war on Asander, and once more captured Panticapaeum, his capital. But in a pitched battle on the open steppe his dismounted Scythians were defeated, since they had never been trained to fight on foot. Pharnaces was killed, fighting in the front rank, in the fifty-first year of his age and the sixteenth of his reign in Bosporus.

So ended the dynasty of Mithradates. The lord of such a prolific harem must have left other children, but they made no mark in the world and are unknown to history.

Pontus remained obedient to Rome, and later to Constantinople, until it was overrun by the Turks at the end of the eleventh century. Bosporus was part of the Roman empire until the Tartars conquered it in the thirteenth century. When Catherine the Great added the Crimea to the Russian empire her cultured ministers, recalling its Greek origins, gave to the towns they founded the Greek names of Sebastopol and Theodosia.

Mithradates Eupator deserves to be remembered as that freak of nature, an absolute monarch who improved with age. He occupied his youth in the usual pastimes of Hellenistic royalty: avenging the murder of his father, murdering his brother, shutting up his mother in prison, marrying his sister. In the prime of life he was a Great King according to the pattern admired in his day; a patron of the arts, a keen sportsman, a lover of many women (though not, it would seem, of boys). In old age he taught himself the business of war; and though on the whole he won few victories he did something much more difficult, he kept the loyalty of his men in defeat. His overland march from Pontus to Bosporus would be enough in itself to earn him fame as a great leader of men, and it was only one episode in twenty-five years of war. The joy of Pompeius at the news of his death is the measure of the Roman fear of him.

His character displays many obvious failings: ruthless

cruelty, caprice, and in the management of the great massacre of 88 a measure of sly treachery. But these were in essence the faults of his environment. He was not so cruel as the Roman government, nor so treacherous as most contemporary Kings. Through all his life, and especially through the latter part of it, runs a strong vein of chivalry, most unusual in the first century. He would not buy his own safety by handing over the Roman exiles who trusted in his protection, he relied on the honour of his mercenaries when he gave them a year's pay in advance, he pardoned even those who betrayed him if they acted from loyalty to their immediate lords. Obviously he did not enjoy the thrill of battle, as some great captains have enjoyed it; in the pride of his youth he directed his campaigns from another continent. But when he considered that his duty as King demanded it he led his men from in front, and they followed him with devotion. He lived in honour, and died with pride.

After he was dead the omens of his birth could be explained. As the comet had filled one-quarter of the heavens, outshining the sun, and had then disappeared, so Mithradates had filled the whole east, outshining even Rome; until Fate decided that it was time for him to vanish.

There still remains the unsolved question: how did he come by all that money? The great horseman, the great warrior, must also have been a great administrator. Probably it was better for the human race that Rome should bring Asia into the full communion of the civilization of the Mediterranean; but Rome had no more worthy adversary than the indomitable King of Pontus.

Bibliography

No contemporary wrote a life of Mithradates in Greek or Latin; or if one was written it has not come down to us. In fact no classical author of any period wrote a formal biography of the great King. But it was impossible to write Roman history without mentioning him, and incidental notices occur in several works.

STRABO was a native of Pontus, whose grandfather had fought for Mithradates and later deserted him. Strabo's *Geography* deals at length with the topography of Pontus, and is especially valuable in its description of the great temple-villages.

APPIAN, who flourished under the Antonine Emperors, wrote a *Roman History*, parts of which have survived. It was planned as a history of the wars of Rome, and one book is devoted to the Mithradatic Wars. The author was by profession a lawyer, not a soldier, and he wrote more than 200 years after the event. But other parts of his work can be checked from the contemporary histories of Polybius and Caesar, and he seems in general to have been accurate and careful.

PLUTARCH'S Lives of Sulla, Lucullus, and Pompeius treat of Mithradates incidentally. Plutarch also wrote long after the event, but he was a careful historian who used sources now lost.

MODERN SOURCES

Mithradate Eupator, Roi de Pont, by Theodore Reinach, Paris, 1890, seems to be the only formal biography of Mithradates in existence. The author himself translated it into Germrn.

The Cambridge Ancient History, volume 9, is a valuable summaay. The late Sir William Tarn was expert in Hellenistic military and naval affairs. His book *Hellenistic Military and Naval Developments* appeared in 1930, but many of his most valuable appreciations must be sought in learned periodicals.

Index

Index

Index

Index

Index

Paphlagonia, 18; bequeathed to Pontus, 28; overrun by *M*, 38; again overrun by *M*, 42

Parthians, 13, 20; clumsy diplomatists, 148

Peltasts, their tactics, 50

Pergamum City, 13; captured by *M*, 58; his capital, 60; omen in the theatre, 69; *M* flees from, 84; capital of Roman Asia, 90.

Pergamum, Kingdom of, 13; allied to Rome, 18; bequeathed to Rome, 23; revolt of Aristonicus, 24

Perseus, King of Macedonia, conquered by Rome, 20

Phalanx, tactics discussed, 49

Phanagoria, revolts against *M*, 189; independent, 196; conquered by Pharnaces, 197

Pharnaces, son of *M* and a concubine, plots against *M*, 191; revolts, 192; King of Bosporus, loyal to Rome, 195; conquers Phanagoria, 197; invades Pontus, 197; defeated by Caesar at Zela, 198; killed in battle, 199

Phoenix, Pontic nobleman, does his duty before changing sides, 123

Phrygia, to Pontus, 24; from Pontus, 29

Piraeus, 64; occupied by Archelaus, 68; attacked by Sulla, 72; captured by Sulla, 76

Pirates, 13, 86; allied to *M*, 96; rescue *M*, 117; Pompeius appointed to suppress them, 158; suppressed, 166

Poison, an old Pontic custom. *M* takes a daily dose, 30

Pompeius fights Sertorius in Spain, 100; appointed to suppress the pirates, 158; suppresses them, 166; takes over from Lucullus, 167; besieges *M*, 171; storms *M's* camp, 173; occupies all Pontus, 176; marches to the Caspian, 181; invades Armenia, 183; grants peace to King Tigranes, 184; marches to Arabia, 186; learns of *M's* death, 195; dies, 197

Pomponius, Roman cavalry commander, 124

Pontus, early history, 15; royal house, 14; described, 17

Popilius Laenas, humiliates King Antiochus, 20, 28

Queen, status of in Hellenistic Kingdoms, 15

Rhodes, 13; ally of Rome, 18, 39; *M's* munificence to, 39; defies *M*, 60; besieged, 65; relieved by Lucullus, 80

Rhyndacus river, Pontic defeat at, 115

Rome and the East, 9; attacks Macedonia, 18; conquers Greece, 21; attitude to slaves, 21; neglect of sea power, 35; menaced by Germans, 37; few troops in the East, 41; Social war, 42; Civil war, 60; conquered by Sulla, 70; declares against *M*, 70

Roxana, sister to *M*, 26; death, 132

Sambuca, marine siege-engine, 66, 109, 111

Scythians, 35; *M* marches through their land, 179; sends his daughters to them, 190; fight for Pharnaces, 199

Senate at Rome, foreign policy, 19; accepts Pergamum, 23; will not ratify transfer of Phrygia to Pontus, 27; too numerous to be bribed, 45; did not authorize attack on *M*, 47

Sertorius rules in Spain, 96; treats with *M*, 97, 107; killed, 127

Sinope, 17; *M's* birthplace, 27; rises for *M*, 31; besieged by Romans, 120; taken by Lucullus, 134

Index